CHAMPIONS
OF AMERICAN SPORT

CHAM
OF AMERICAN

Foreword by

The National Portrait Gallery, Smithsonian Institution

.ed Smith

PIONS

SPORT

Written and edited by Marc Pachter
with Amy Henderson, Jeannette Hussey,
and Margaret C. S. Christman

Harry N. Abrams, Inc., Publishers, New York

An exhibition at the National Portrait Gallery, June 23 to
September 7, 1981, made possible in part by a generous grant
from Philip Morris and Miller Brewing Company

Exhibition organized by

Beverly Jones Cox, Curator of Exhibitions
Marc Pachter, Historian
Kenneth A. Yellis, Curator of Education

Nello Marconi, Chief, Exhibition Design and Production
Frances Stevenson Wein, Editor
Marvin Sadik, Director

Exhibition Itinerary:

The Chicago Historical Society	Fall 1981
The California Museum of Science and Industry, Los Angeles	Winter 1982
The American Museum of Natural History, New York	Spring 1982

Robert Morton, Project Director
Donn Teal, Editor; Darilyn Lowe, Designer

Library of Congress Cataloging in Publication Data

Pachter, Marc.
Champions of American sport.

"[Catalog of] an exhibition at the National
Portrait Gallery, June 23 to September 7, 1981,
sponsored by Philip Morris Incorporated."
1. Athletes—United States—Portraits—
Exhibitions. 2. Athletes—United States—Biog-
raphy. 3. Washington, D.C.—Exhibitions.
4. National Portrait Gallery, Washington, D.C.
—Exhibitions. I. National Portrait Gallery,
Washington, D.C. II. Philip Morris Incorporated.
III. Title.
GV697.A1P28   796′092′2 [B]   80–28934
ISBN 0–8109–1602–9 (Abrams)   AACR1
ISBN 0–8109–2250–9 (Abrams: pbk.)

SPONSOR'S STATEMENT

Buy me some peanuts and crackerjack,
I don't care if I never get back . . .

. . . from the exhibition of outstanding American sports heroes and heroines of the past century and more, mounted by the National Portrait Gallery of the Smithsonian Institution. These heroes and heroines, with the legions of athletic idols they typify, occupy a special place in our lives and in our national psyche. To watch what they did so superbly could be called a form of social escape—but not entirely; and the exhibition does not seek mere outbursts of instant nostalgia for heroes and events vividly recalled, or vaguely remembered, or perhaps never even known.

Sports is lively, always contemporary and active. It is play and shared fun and then more: group drama, mass entertainment, community spectacle, politics. It is a feature of the times, inextricably woven into the tapestry of American life. From our days as colonies inching toward independence, the spirit of American sports has been an integral part of the American spirit. For many, rooting for the home team and the local athlete was our first conscious exercise in group belonging and patriotism.

Philip Morris Incorporated, through its corporate support of art, has helped to mine our country's rich lode of history for insights into our national traits. We have sponsored major exhibitions that have traveled through the United States—and, often, around the world—pertaining to American Indians, Western art, black art, women, native folk art, and children. Now, in the National Portrait Gallery, we support a show about the world of sports and one hundred of its great figures. Philip Morris and Miller Brewing Company are honored to be associated with this exhibition. Long before any of us joined the company, we, like almost everyone else, were committed fans of the greats of sports.

Perhaps what we Americans like best about our sports idols is that we created them with our own zest and enthusiasm. They *belong* to us; we revel in their glory, take possession of their triumph, and hold them as trophies in our collective memory. In the arena, on the track, wherever they play at whatever they play, they are our designated surrogates performing the impossible, striving for perfection and often achieving it. They are just like us, only more so: eleven feet tall and strong, fearless, fleet, keen of eye, daring, and unbeatable.

This exhibition is one of a kind, and we are glad we came to the game.

George Weissman
Chairman of the Board
Philip Morris Incorporated

CONTENTS

ACKNOWLEDGMENTS

The idea behind this exhibition of sports heroes and heroines did not originally come from the three of us who have organized it but rather from one of the staff's most avid sports fans, our former Curator of Education, Dennis O'Toole. Acutely aware of the lack of athletes represented in our permanent collection, he saw such an exhibition as focusing the National Portrait Gallery's attention on the figures who have so captured the American imagination. Our only regret is that he was not here to work with us; we hope that the result measures up to his inspiration.

We had little idea of what lay ahead of us when we began. We were sure that our foray into uncharted territory would be an adventure, but beyond that, because of the virtual omnipresence of sports, we guessed that our task might be simple. Only after we were well on our way did we truly confront the vastness—in every sense of the word—of our project. Such a gargantuan undertaking would never have been possible without the help and, indeed, the instruction of a great many people.

First of all, we would like to thank the champions themselves who took the time to work with us: Kareem Abdul-Jabbar, Dick Button, Don Budge, Sandy Koufax, Ted Williams, Bob Mathias, O. J. Simpson, Arnold Palmer, Gale Sayers, Patty Berg, Larry Mahan, Pancho Gonzales, Jim Ryun, Emil Mosbacher, Peggy Fleming, Eric Heiden, George Halas, Willie Mays, Joe DiMaggio, Hank Luisetti, Bob Cousy, Jack Kramer, and Bill Russell.

Many of the champions' families, too, were of great help, literally going through scrapbooks and boxes to find appropriate material. Our special thanks go to Mrs. Janet Camp Troxell, Nadine Kahanamoku, Mrs. Dominic Pirone, Mrs. Vince Lombardi, August Belmont IV, John A. Fitzsimmons, Mrs. R. D. Beckworth, Mrs. William Van Lengen, Mrs. Jackie Robinson, Mrs. Maxine Halprin, and Grace and Gail Thorpe. Lou and Monica Marciano, and Peter Marciano, gathered material from the whole family for us to select from.

Early in our research, we were fortunate to meet Bill Goff of Spectrum Fine Art Gallery in New York. Bill has made sports art his life, and he not only opened his collection to us but gave us names of artists and collectors in the field. Each visit with him brought new leads for us to pursue. It was a genuine pleasure to work with someone so willing to give of his time.

Germaine Glidden, Director and Founder of the National Art Museum of Sport, now in New Haven, Connecticut, brought out files from past exhibitions and allowed us to take advantage of research that the Museum had sponsored.

Sports Illustrated was a welcome ally. Richard Gangel, Art Director, who has a well-deserved reputation for fostering sports art, and his assistant Jo Schiano—one of those people without whom you wonder how anything could get done—were most helpful. John Dominis, Picture Editor, Nancy Kirkland, Director of Picture Sales, and Robert Taylor, Picture Librarian, were immensely kind and patient. A large number of photographs from their superb collection—representing the finest photographers working in sports—are reproduced in the catalogue and exhibition.

The staffs of the various halls of fame, knowing that we were all in the same game, were generous with their time and advice. No exhibition dealing with baseball could ever be mounted, or book written, without the assistance of the Baseball Hall of Fame at Cooperstown, New York. Howard Talbot, its Director, Peter Clark, its Curator, and William J. Guilfoile, its Public Relations Agent, gave us complete access to the collection there. Our visits to the Ring Boxing Hall of Fame in New York City and its inimitable President, Bert Sugar, will always be remembered. Colonel Robert S. Day of the Tennis Hall of Fame in Newport, Rhode Island, answered almost daily calls from us with incredible patience. Janet Seagle, Librarian of Golf House in Far Hills, New Jersey, did the same. We are grateful to Elaine Mann, Director of the National Racing Hall of Fame in Saratoga Springs, New York, for her warm hospitality and for introducing us to the racing world and its vernacular. Other halls of fame were equally helpful: Buck Dawson, Director, and Donna Levie, Librarian, at the International Swimming Hall of Fame in Fort Lauderdale, Florida; Lee Williams, Director, Basketball Hall of Fame, Springfield, Massachusetts; William Schroeder, Citizens Savings Athletic Foundation, Los Angeles; Jack Martin, Director, and Al Bloemker, Vice President, of the Indianapolis Speedway Museum; Joe Horrigan, Curator, Pro Football Hall of Fame, Canton, Ohio; Bob Eidson, General Manager, Professional Rodeo Cowboys Association; Thomas E. Hall, Executive Director, Ice Skating Institute of America; and Jerry McGaha and Helen Cataldi, United States Figure Skating Association.

The following individuals also extended a helping hand: David W. Muir, Francis Ouimet Caddie Scholarship Fund; Sohei Hohri, Librarian, New York Yacht Club; Brian Walker, Director, Museum of Cartoon Art; Jim Jacobs of Big Fights, Inc.; William J. Maher, University of Illinois Archives; Herbert T. Juliano, International Sport and Game Collections, Notre Dame University; C. Robert Paul, Communications Director, United States Olympic Committee; Mrs. Georgetta van Buitenen, Director, and Mrs. Betty Wendland, Assistant to the Director, World Heritage Museum, University of Illinois; Rudy Custer, Business Manager, Chicago Bears; Jeremy Chisholm, Director, Chisholm Gallery in Palm Beach, Florida; Eugene T. Branch and Frances M. Bird of the Jones, Bird and Howell law offices in Atlanta; Trudy Hanson, Larry Viskochil, and Archie Motley of the Chicago Historical Society; Tim Peterson, Indiana Historical Society; Steven Miller, Museum of the City of New York; and Eva S. Auchincloss, Executive Director, Women's Sports

Foundation. Pryor Dodge gave us valuable information about bicycle collections in Europe. Closer to home, we want to thank Carl Scheele and Ellen Hughes of the Department of Community Life, National Museum of American History, who have assembled the beginnings of a sports collection within the Smithsonian, and Douglas Evelyn, Deputy Director, and Don Berkebile, Associate Curator of the Division of Transportation, National Museum of American History.

Without the artists and photographers who have captured the images of our sports legends and their great moments, we would have been helpless. It is a pleasure to acknowledge the cooperation of Daniel Schwartz, Joe Brown, John Groth, Don Moss, Rhoda Sherbell, Robert Handville, Malcolm Alexander, Harold Castor, Merv Corning, Ralph Fasanella, Richard Stone Reeves, Duane Hanson, Stanley Rosenfeld, Neil Leifer, Fred Kaplan, Robert Riger, Jeanne Moutoussamy-Ashe, Vernon Biever, Nate Fine, and Ken Regan.

Several private collections were opened to us, and their contributions have been vital to our project. Dr. and Mrs. Daniel Turner enthusiastically showed us their baseball and boxing collection. Joel Platt, who has long dreamed of creating a Sports Immortals Museum, has lovingly put together a collection of memorabilia encompassing all sports, and in so doing has preserved for all time objects important to our national heritage. We are deeply indebted to him.

Various people on the National Portrait Gallery staff contributed their expertise and assistance. William Stapp offered his counsel on bicycle racing, Ellen Miles provided advice on winter sports, and Wendy Wick helped us find several rare sporting prints. The catalogue text was reviewed by Frances Stevenson Wein and was typed through each of its stages by Eloise P. Harvey. Eugene Mantie and Rolland White handled a heavy volume of special photography requirements. David Schwarz, Sarah Cash, and Margot Roddy worked indefatigably to collect the photographs and handle the myriad details of organizing the exhibition.

Beverly Cox
Marc Pachter
Ken Yellis

FOREWORD

It is a regrettable fact of life on the racetrack that "Are they trying?" is sometimes a valid question, though not necessarily diplomatic. It is asked because once in a while a horse will be put in a race where he doesn't belong, and the jockey will be advised to have a nice ride and get home at his leisure. This is done for mysterious reasons, best known to those involved, but just possibly having something to do with getting better odds on the horse next time out.

These observations are prompted by the appearance of James Fitzsimmons and Eddie Arcaro in this book as entries. James Fitzsimmons, known in the newspapers as "Sunny Jim" but usually addressed as "Mr. Fitz," was an ornament on the thoroughbred scene for most of a century. On the day of Grover Cleveland's first inauguration as President, young Jim got a job as exercise rider at the Sheepshead Bay track on Long Island.

He rode races at tracks like St. Asaph, Gloucester, Alexander Island, and others lost to memory. He also rode night races on Long Island not many decades after Edison had invented the incandescent light. One night he drove his horse to the edge of exhaustion, trying to shake off a challenger that turned out to be his own shadow, with no other horses within lengths.

When he grew too heavy to ride, he turned to training horses, and for more than fifty years his cheerful patience, his sweet humor, and his matchless skill enriched that field. In all that time, he never posed for a formal photograph. Indeed, he didn't even make the winner's circle pictures when Gallant Fox, one of his two Triple Crown winners, captured the Kentucky Derby. A state trooper wouldn't let this stooped, apologetic little man cross the track to join his horse.

He was well along in his eighties when his family took him by force to a photographic studio in Sheepshead Bay. A pair of sportswriters happened to be visiting his quarters at old Aqueduct when the finished work was delivered, and he inscribed a picture for each of them. It was delightful. It showed him in his Sunday suit with a hard collar, and he was smiling up at the camera through the tops of his eyes.

"Gee, Mr. Fitz," a visitor said, "this is great, perfect! Thank you."

Mr. Fitz had resisted visiting the photographer, but now he was pleased with the result. It brought out the old jockey in him. "I was really trying that time," he said.

When Eddie Arcaro was the best jockey of his time, a tale was told that may be apocryphal. In those days the opportunity to abuse Arcaro was one of the attractions that drew customers to the New York tracks, especially Aqueduct and Jamaica. Because of Eddie's reputation, many players backed his mounts indiscriminately, sometimes sending one off at even money when, on form and ability, he shouldn't be better than 3 to 1. When the horse lost, as he did often enough because Arcaro couldn't ride faster than the horse could run, Eddie's public booed the pants off him.

He took the abuse, but he resented it. Toney Betts of the New York *Mirror* tried to console him. "You're a public performer, Eddie, and you have to take the bad with the good, the boos with the cheers. It happens to everybody. Out at Yankee Stadium, you know, they boo Joe DiMaggio."

Eddie was aghast. "They do?" he said. "But he's *always* trying!"

Arcaro and Mr. Fitz are only two of the sports figures celebrated in these pages. There are stories about all the others, but there's not enough space to tell them in an introduction. Not that I know all that much, for that matter, about Hiram Woodruff, the whiskery dean of harness racing in the early nineteenth century; John C. Stevens, who brought the Hundred Guinea Cup of the Royal Yacht Squadron to the United States, where it became the America's Cup; Arthur Zimmerman, world champion cyclist in 1893; or Jackson Haines, the pioneer of figure skating.

Yet they were all genuine celebrities in their day.

So far as is known, the National Portrait Gallery's show is the first major exhibition ever devoted entirely to sports heroes. High time, too, for sports are as much a part of our civilization as banks, law courts, and churches. In any culture we know anything about, sports have commanded wide interest; among the monuments of ancient Rome still standing, the largest and most imposing is the stadium that housed Rome's bravest gladiators and hungriest lions.

Champions of American Sport is a companion piece to the exhibition, intended to supplement and expand on the images displayed, but for sprightly writing on subjects that command lively and sustained interest, the book can easily stand on its own. From the lordly Mike "King" Kelly of Boston baseball in the era of silk hats and patent-leather mustaches to the flamboyant Muhammad Ali, these sketches provide delightful reading about extraordinary individuals.

Read and rejoice.

W. W. (Red) Smith

INTRODUCTION

America has paid tribute to her sports heroes in the stadium, the media, and even on the backs of bubble gum cards. The National Portrait Gallery of the Smithsonian Institution offers a deeper dimension of tribute: an exhibition devoted to the great sports personalities our country has produced—from the early days when boxing was illegal, track an entertainment for county fairs, and baseball a brawling newborn, to our own Golden Age of athletic achievement. This is the first major sports exhibition ever mounted by the nation. It spotlights the men and women who—just like the politicians, the generals, the artists—have shaped our sense of ourselves and, in a special way, have lent color to our lives and reaffirmed our faith in what the individual can do.

We need our myths, our legends. What other field has produced so many? Joe Di-Maggio at home plate, Willie Shoemaker in the saddle, John L. Sullivan in the ring, Jesse Owens and Wilma Rudolph on the track, Jim Thorpe and Babe Didrikson expressing their physical genius in countless feats of endurance and skill. In a nation as diverse as ours, who has not heard of coach Knute Rockne; or Babe Ruth, "The Sultan of Swat"; or Johnny "Tarzan" Weissmuller, who swam before he swung; or Ben Hogan or Sonja Henie? And who, fifty years from now, will not have heard of Muhammad Ali or Billie Jean King? These are figures whose lives have left a special resonance in our memory, charismatic men and women who fascinate and inspire.

We also aim to breathe life back into several legends in eclipse: Isaac Murphy, the greatest jockey of the nineteenth century, until blacks ceased to dominate the field; Edward Payson Weston, a walker of epic spirit who met every challenge, including a punishing stride across the nation at age seventy; Mike "King" Kelly, the first baseball hero to win adulation and, in the process, a popular song, "Slide Kelly Slide"; and Jackson Haines, the nineteenth-century dancer-turned-ice-skater who was the first great figure skater, shaping the sport during his long stay abroad. With these stand figures outside the competitive arena who were nevertheless great sportsmen: the legendary boxing promoter Tex Rickard, the horse trainer James "Sunny Jim" Fitzsimmons, the umpire Bill Klem (with his satisfying sour face), and the brilliant baseball commissioner and curmudgeon Kenesaw Mountain Landis.

Americans of every imaginable stripe come together as fans. This book, we hope, will appeal to all of them. It will appeal, also, to both children and adults: sports is one of the few points where the interests of the generations truly join. And with good reason. The athletes whose personalities and careers are evoked here by paintings, sculpture, prints, and photographs satisfy a universal need for heroes. Their blend of raw talent and relentless discipline reminds us of what the body and spirit can accomplish.

We understand all too well how many great sports figures the nation has produced and regret how few of them we have the space to include in our sampling. Where, for example, are Stan Musial, the legendary St. Louis slugger; or Maureen Connolly, tennis champion; or Mendy Rudolph, prince of basketball referees; or Sam Snead, of the glorious golf swing; or Tom Harmon, football great of Michigan? Where are they and hundreds of others who gave their times a reason to cheer? Our answer can only be—and we ourselves feel the pang of the omissions—that we have not tried to define an ultimate list of one hundred American sports heroes and heroines (can one ever be made?), but to suggest an *overview* of many eras, sports styles, and roles on and off the field. We cannot include all of America's champions, so we have tried to make our few suggest the greatness of all.

The making of sports heroes is an American tradition we seek to reflect, not explain. Certain sports—baseball and football above all—have produced more nationally recognized figures than others; and so their contingents here are large. Other sports have come in for broad-based national attention only through the force of character of a particular individual, such as polo's Tommy Hitchcock; and we have tried to reflect that as well. We find, too, that certain eras have produced more than their fair share of champions—preeminently the Twenties and our own second Golden Age of Sport. Whether this is because greater numbers of superb players have bunched in one generation or another, or only because the nation was more willing to watch and reward them at those times, is a riddle worthy of the chicken and the egg. We cannot answer it, but we have allowed those eras sway in our final selection. And, finally, we have been influenced, too, by the disproportionate attention lavished on certain positions within a sport—and the personalities attracted to these positions. It is, above all, the sluggers and the heavyweights who fill the arenas and inspire the sportswriters. Americans are stirred by offense more than by defense, by aggressive power more than by patient strategy, by leaders more than by supportive players, by all-or-nothing winners more than by good losers. These are the athletes who crowd our selection.

Brought together here are some of the most dramatic and exhilarating individuals our society has produced. Their magic is hard to define but unmistakable. This, then, is not a history of dates, of all-inclusive events, of encyclopedic completeness; rather, it is a celebration of certain lives and their power to move us. It is, above all, a tribute to the heroic tradition of sports as a domain of the American imagination.

Marc Pachter

CHAMPIONS

OF AMERICAN SPORT

Night Game (Practice Time), Ralph Fasanella, Oil on canvas, 1979, Collection of the artist

BASEBALL

Biographies by
MARC PACHTER

A nineteenth-century sports song cover, 1867, Library of Congress

Below:
Baseball Players Practicing,
Thomas Eakins, Watercolor, 1875,
Museum of Art, Rhode Island School
of Design, Jesse Metcalfe Fund and
Walter H. Kimball Fund

The Baseball Player, Samuel A. Robb,
Polychromed wood, 1888/1903,
Heritage Plantation of Sandwich,
Massachusetts

Right:
Champion's Choice, Leo Jensen,
Mixed-media construction, 1963
Spectrum Fine Art Gallery,
New York City

21

MIKE "KING" KELLY (1857–1894)

Boston already had a barrel-chested, mustachioed, hard-drinking sports hero when Mike Kelly came to town in 1887. But there was room in New England hearts for yet another. Like "The Great John L." Sullivan, "King" Kelly was a showman as well as an athlete. Brilliant in his London silk hat, his ascot set off by jewels, and his patent-leather shoes, he looked like anything but a baseball player as he strutted about the city followed by legions of admirers. The first true idol of the diamond, Kelly dressed and drank like a lord and was treated accordingly. When the "cranks"—as fans were then called—presented him with a fine carriage in which to ride to the playing field, he accepted it as only his due.

Kelly came heralded by baseball's biggest contract to date. Veteran of a great career of seven seasons with the Chicago White Stockings, he had been sold for what Chicagoans bitterly called "ten thousand dollars in Puritanic gold" and was offered an unprecedented $5,000-a-year salary. The wags immediately dubbed him "The Ten-Thousand-Dollar Beauty," after the actress Louise Montagne. But Mike was worth every cent. In his first ten days with the Boston Nationals, he made more hits, stole more bases, and scored more runs than any of his teammates.

So impressive was Kelly's hitting style that the Chicago poet Eugene Field, witness of his 1886 year as the top batter in the country, coined a word to describe it. Others might merely "pound or buffet, knock or swipe" the ball, but Kelly's swing, reasoned the poet, caused

22

such worry among the opposition that "swat"—an old word for sweat—poured out. His opponents also had something else to fear. Kelly virtually created the art form of the slide. Perched at first base, Kelly could count on the stands erupting with pleading to "slide, Kelly, slide" until he made his crowd-pleasing bid. Dashing toward second or third base, he would squirm and wiggle his way to safety, leaving the addled baseman no more than a finger or toe to touch. "Oh it's slide, Kelly, slide,/And it's slide, Mike, slide," sang out *chanteuse* Maggie Kline in a popular song of the day. "For there's oil upon the skirt/Of his woollen undershirt/When he takes his little hand sled for a slide."

Star of baseball's anarchic period, Kelly—who had joined the Cincinnati Red Stockings in 1878, only nine years after its formation as the first major-league team—played the game according to his own free interpretation of the rules. When the field's lone umpire was distracted, "Kel" rarely bothered to go near second base on a direct run from first to third. His most notorious bending of the rules happened in 1890, when he was player-manager in the short-lived Players' League. Sitting on the bench as a foul tip came his way, he leaped up, announced, "Kelly now catching for Boston," and made the game-winning catch. It was technically legal but hardly in the spirit of the substitution rule. Kelly's lasting monument was a change in the books which stipulated that substitutions could not be made while a game was in progress.

A better actor on the field than on the stage, Kelly made a few poor attempts at vaudeville drama during off-season. His fans tolerated, even rejoiced in, the bad acting as long as his athletic prowess sustained their interest, but Kelly's career and life began to slide in the early 1890s. Years of drinking gave him a bad case of "brandy-legs" and the irritating habit of falling over himself during a crucial play. In 1893 Boston, fed up, lent him to the New York Giants, who suspended him for passing up too many pre-game sobering Turkish baths. Cast out into the wilds of the minor leagues, he caught pneumonia in 1894 and died soon after. Sensing one last opportunity for melodrama, the magnificent Kelly, it is said, whispered at the end, "This is my last slide."

Far left:
Mike "King" Kelly,
Boston Public Library

Medal given to "King" Kelly by a Boston fan,
1888, National Baseball
Hall of Fame and Museum,
Inc., Cooperstown, New York

TY COBB (1886–1961)

Ty Cobb proved that you do not have to be loved to be a baseball star. You may even be cordially hated—by the thousands of fans who crowd the stands to watch and heckle, by teammates who seethe with resentment, and by opponents who are plainly afraid. But, to pull it off, you have to be very good, and "The Georgia Peach" certainly was—so good that he seemed possessed by the furies as he rounded the bases, so good that he closed the record books forever in a number of categories, so good that a fascinated world recognized him for a genius, one of the two greatest baseball players ever.

Fans will always dispute whether Babe Ruth or Cobb deserves the ultimate accolade. But it's a comparison of apples and peaches. Each mastered a completely different era. Before Ruth swatted in the age of hitting power, baseball was a confined game of strategy and maneuver—and no one maneuvered better than Ty Cobb. The game that he knew was shaped by the use of the "deadball"—far heavier than the cork-centered sphere which Ruth and his contemporaries belted out of the park. Fans of the early twentieth century didn't expect home runs. What they came to see was a duel between pitcher and batter, runner and baseman. No sudden miracles would carry the day, only the steady accumulation of hits, runs, and stolen bases. Victory went to the swiftest, the shrewdest, the hungriest team.

Lean, mean-eyed Cobb—so unlike pudgy Babe Ruth—knew how to stare down a pitcher and unsettle an entire field. No one knocked out more hits—4,191 in 11,429 times at bat—and probably no one ever will. Over twenty-two years of play for the Detroit Tigers, from 1905 to 1926, and two more for the Philadelphia Athletics, ending his career in 1928, Cobb became immortal. In the 1936 voting for the first five inductees into the Baseball Hall of Fame, he was easily first, winning an astonishing total of 222 out of 226 votes.

A Ty Cobb souvenir fan,
National Baseball Hall of
Fame and Museum, Inc.,
Cooperstown, New York

Cobb sliding, National Baseball Hall of Fame and Museum, Inc., Cooperstown, New York

Cobb's secret was no true secret at all. He shouted it to the winds in his contempt for all the halfhearted, overspecialized players in his, and later, generations. They practiced often; he practiced by the hour, bunting, throwing, sliding until he was raw. They accepted their limitations; he had to be good at everything. They wanted to win; he *had* to win. That need communicated itself as meanness. Few were so adept at inspiring fear. Once he announced that he would "cut the heart out of my best friend if he ever tried to block the road." No one who ever saw Cobb's shoe-spikes flash as he sped around the diamond or witnessed the damage they could inflict on a too-slow third baseman as Cobb came in feet first doubted his determination.

Above all, Cobb was a master psychologist with a sixth sense for knowing the other fellow's weakness. Taunting a pitcher or sitting on the bench slyly sharpening his spikes, he created a mood of excitement and suspense which he and the stadium crowds seemed to relish. Rarely was he out of control. Once a cursing fan provoked him to charge the stands, drawing blood from his tormentor. But usually the anger stayed bottled within, fueling the demons which drove him on to glory. There has never been another competitor like him in baseball, or perhaps in the history of American sport. He was, wrote baseball's most spirited writer, Ring Lardner, "Tyrus the Greatest."

25

Christy Mathewson, James F. Kernan, Oil on canvas, Date unknown, Keystone Junior College, LaPlume, Pennsylvania

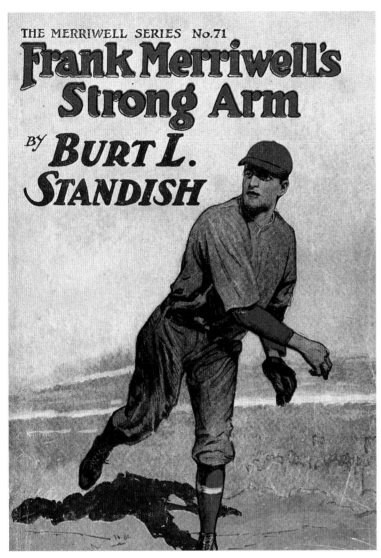

America found a true-life Frank Merriwell—boy-hero of the dime novel—in pitcher Mathewson, Ohio State University Libraries

Mathewson warming up, National Portrait Gallery, Smithsonian Institution

CHRISTY MATHEWSON (1880–1925)

No one American athlete, in any sport, has ever summed up the values of his era more than did Christy Mathewson, pitcher. This "Greek God in flannels," as the publicists liked to call him, appeared on the major-league diamond, during the first years of the twentieth century, as if in answer to the national yearning for a gentleman-hero. Every boy who thrilled to the dime-novel adventures of young Dink Stover or Frank Merriwell of Yale had a living model in "Matty," more than six feet tall, tousled blond hair, well-mannered, and college-educated. He had gone to Bucknell instead of Merriwell's Yale, but that was close enough at a time when few players had been to college at all. Baseball gloried in its rough-necked, hard-drinking, roustabout spirit when Mathewson first stepped upon its muddy fields. "He handed the game," wrote dean of sportswriters Grantland Rice, "a certain . . . indefinable lift in culture, brains, personality."

Mathewson would be remembered today even if he had lacked those golden attributes of body and spirit. At a point when baseball was a pitcher's game, dominated by such

27

immortals as Walter Johnson, Grover Cleveland Alexander, Chief Bender, and Rube Waddell, Mathewson's strong right arm made him a star second to none. Over a period of sixteen full seasons of play with the New York Giants, he won twenty or more games thirteen years and thirty or more games four years. In 1908 he pitched his team to victory a record-making thirty-seven times. But Christy would be on the books for no other reason than his performance at the legendary World Series of 1905 against the Philadelphia Athletics. All five games pitched were shutouts, three of them Mathewson's. His first victory, 3–0, he allowed only four hits; his second, 9–0, he allowed four again; his third, 2–0, he gave out six. Throughout all three games, only one man walked, and only one man reached third. It would be counted the greatest World Series pitching ever seen.

"Big Six"—as he was nicknamed when a writer compared him to New York's famous horse-drawn fire engine—was a specialist in victories, but not in strikeouts. To save his arm, he took it easy, getting a batter out any way he could. But he poured on the steam, like the engine "Big Six," when it mattered. Matty was happiest when he was "pitching in a pinch," as he titled his book. That was when the batters got a good look at his famous "fadeaway." It was a curve ball in reverse that broke suddenly down toward the right-handed hitter and away from the left-handed hitter. To the helpless man on deck, it looked like a fastball that just faded away.

Surprisingly, the golden boy of baseball developed a reputation for hard luck. On one occasion, teammate Fred Merkle failed to touch second base in a game that would have rounded off Matty's best season, in 1908, with a pennant win. Other Giants were persuaded that they had seen Merkle touch, but Mathewson, characteristically honest, confirmed the umpire's ruling, leading to a play-off game he was too exhausted to win. Four years later, "Snodgrass's Muff" lost the World Series for Mathewson when the outfielder failed to catch an easy fly. These disappointments were minor, however, next to the central tragedy of his life. One of a number of baseball players to volunteer for service in World War I, he returned from France with his lungs weakened by poison gas and then came down with tuberculosis. After recuperation in a sanitarium, he decided to return to baseball as president of the Boston Braves. That decision cost him his life. After a relapse brought on by overwork, he was dead at forty-five.

Pitching in a Pinch, *by Christy Mathewson (Boy Scout edition),* National Baseball Hall of Fame and Museum, Inc., Cooperstown, New York

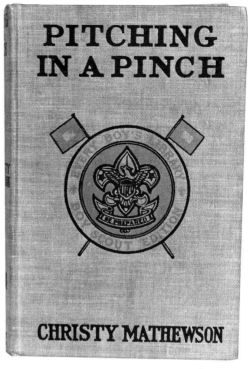

Christy Mathewson, Gertrude Boyle, Bronze, c. 1915/20, National Baseball Hall of Fame and Museum, Inc., Cooperstown, New York

KENESAW MOUNTAIN LANDIS (1866–1944)

It was just like Kenesaw Mountain Landis, judge of the federal court of Chicago in 1920, to keep a delegation of baseball club owners waiting anxiously until he found the time to see them. Wrapped tightly in the mantle of his invincible virtue, he knew that they had come to offer him the newly minted position of commissioner of baseball, and he knew, too, that he could have the position on his own terms. These he spelled out as soon as he granted the magnates an audience. The judge would accept the $50,000-a-year position (he was then making $7,500) only on condition that he be granted virtually unlimited power to regulate the game. He would welcome the advice of the owners, but under no circumstances could they overrule his decision. They agreed, and baseball enthroned what one writer called "the only successful dictator in United States history."

The assembled club owners, a group not known for its meekness, had little recourse but to accept Landis's absolute leadership. Confidence in the national game was, in 1920, at an all-time low, and its top organization was in disarray. Rumors that the surprise defeat of the Chicago White Sox in the 1919 World Series had been fixed by New York gamblers led to a grand jury investigation and confessions by a number of Chicago players, branded the "Black Sox." The game's top management was in no position to deal with the crisis. The National Commission, which had ruled since 1903, had lost its third member, and the two remaining, presidents of the American and National Leagues, could not agree on a replacement.

Enter Landis. Although the frantic club owners, who feared the loss of value in their franchises, considered asking General Pershing or William Howard Taft to lead them through their crisis, Judge Landis proved the obvious choice. Famous for his pronouncements against crooked big business, he had become a national figure in 1907 when he summoned John D. Rockefeller to his courtroom and fined Standard Oil of Indiana $29,240,000 for paying illegal rebates. The good judge, his rectitude set off by a shock of white hair and matching high, stiff, puritanical collar, was the very image of fearless incorruptibility that baseball so desperately needed.

There was strength behind his style. Determined to purge baseball of any suggestion of wrongdoing, he ignored the dismissal of charges against the Black Sox (their confessions had mysteriously disappeared and were then repudiated) and passed his own, unbending judgment, banishing them from the game forever: "Regardless of the verdict of juries, no player who throws a ball game, no player who entertains proposals or promises to throw a ball game, no player who sits in conference with a bunch of crooked players and does not promptly tell his club about it will ever again play professional baseball." It was a high-minded and high-handed position that no modern court would sustain. But Landis did what he was hired to do, and the scandal was put to rest.

In the course of his near-quarter-century tenure, "Integrity Mountain" took on everyone who challenged his authority. The mighty Babe Ruth, warned not to go on a barnstorming tour after the 1921 World Series, barked: "What has that long-haired old goat to do with me?"—and found out when Landis suspended him for the first forty days of the 1922 season against the protest of the Yankee owners. The whole breed of owners groaned their protest when Landis granted free agency to a number of young players bound by contracts he considered unfair. Going against Landis seemed a challenge to the national game itself—an impression he always underscored by showing up in countless photographs eating hot dogs, throwing out balls, or just lending grandfatherly dignity to the gatherings of baseball players. He was a photogenic public-relations genius, second only to Santa Claus in the national affection. The columnist Heywood Broun summed him up best: "His career typifies the heights to which dramatic talent may carry a man in America if only he has the foresight not to go on the stage."

◀ *Kenesaw Mountain Landis in 1919,* Chicago Historical Society

Babe Ruth,
Nickolas Muray,
Photograph, c. 1927,
National Portrait Gallery,
Smithsonian Institution

Opposite:
Ruth was awarded
this crown when
he was titled
"Sultan of Swat,"
National Baseball
Hall of Fame
and Museum, Inc.,
Cooperstown,
New York

BABE RUTH (1895–1948)

Babe Ruth was the ultimate hero of a sport with more than its fair share of heroes—a giant of monumental swagger and breathtaking talent who set the standard by which all others would be judged. Sportswriters competed to glorify his name and his strong arm. He was "The Sultan of Swat," "The Colossus of Clout," "The Behemoth of Bust," "The Bambino," and "The Slambino." To find his like, writers reached back into myth. Grantland Rice called his achievement "Homeric, no pun intended." Paul Gallico pronounced him "an American Porthos, a swashbuckler built on gigantic and heroic lines." Heywood Broun, reporting the 1923 World Series, crafted the most famous opening sentence in baseball journalism to celebrate his elemental force: "The Ruth is mighty and shall prevail."

The first rumblings of greatness came out of New England in 1919. George Herman Ruth, of the Boston Red Sox, had already made his name in four full seasons as a superb southpaw pitcher, boasting a record twenty-nine scoreless consecutive innings in World Series competition. But that was all prelude. Switched to the outfield, he logged, that historic year, twenty-nine homers—sensational at a time when good players managed no more than twelve. Ruth had hung out his shingle as baseball's first specialist in home runs. It was a new ball game.

A few skeptics remained in 1920 when the Yankees paid the Red Sox $125,000 for Ruth—a figure later to rank as a bargain with the purchase of Manhattan. For the time it was an enormous sum, based on what might have been a fluke year. Ruth silenced the critics with an astonishing fifty-four homers his first Yankee season and fifty-nine the next, each one delivered with a satisfying wallop that resounded in the national imagination. He was an answered prayer for a game reeling from the shock effects of the Black Sox scandal. Commissioner Landis restored baseball's moral authority, but it was the Babe's authority with the bat that brought the fans flocking back. Attendance records were broken, profits soared, and players' salaries chased—at a respectful distance—Ruth's rise to a peak of $80,000 in 1930. (Told that President Hoover made only $75,000, the Babe snorted, "Yeah, but I had a better year than he did.") When the Yankees—once poor cousins to the New York Giants—moved into their grand new Bronx stadium in 1923, the nation knew it as "The House That Ruth Built."

The Babe did not do it all single-handedly. He had a supporting cast of Bronx Bombers, adding up by 1927—when they finished nineteen games ahead of the second-place Philadelphia Athletics—to the most devastating team in history. But it was Ruth and his war club that everyone came to worship. At the prospect of each new Ruthian homer, the fans would become "so crazy with excitement," remembered the great pitcher Walter Johnson, "that they were ready to tear apart the stands [even] when the game was already won, and there was nothing particular at stake." The mighty Bambino could get as much mileage out of a strikeout—he managed a record 1,330—as out of a solid hit. The force of his all-or-nothing swing, twirling his bear's body around those spindly legs, had a glory all its own. Few men were as spectacular in success as he was in failure.

Ruth never did things halfway, on or off the field. His carousing was legendary, his gluttony staggering. Once, in 1925, an overload of hot dogs and soda pop brought on "the bellyache heard round the world," a case of acute indigestion which nearly killed him. But usually he got away with his style of life. And that was the wonder of the man. Out all night, he would show up at the ball park and put away those home runs with a cocky disregard for mere human limitations. Above all men, he seemed master of his own fate. Ruth's go-for-broke spirit reached its peak in the 1932 World Series when, after a session of razzing from his opponents with two strikes down, he confidently pointed in the direction of center field and sent a homer flying just as he had called it. People still argue about whether he had really planned the feat. But Ruth's joyful trot around the bases left no doubt in the minds of the cheering fans.

Ruth's career ended, after fifteen Yankee seasons, in 1934, followed by a sad, short season of declining power with the Boston Braves. No other man's ghost has so dominated a sport. "It will be a long time before any slugger breaks his all-time home run mark of 714," wrote Grantland Rice after Ruth's death of cancer in 1948. "And at the risk of sounding disloyal to the game, I hope it's an eternity before some youngster . . . smashes Babe's mark the 60 homers in one season." Some things are sacred.

Ruth autographs baseballs for his fans, Culver Pictures

Right:
The House That Ruth Built: *Yankee Stadium,* Burris Jenkins, Pen-and-ink cartoon, c. 1934, National Baseball Hall of Fame and Museum, Inc., Cooperstown, New York

Ruth's last appearance in Yankee Stadium—June 13, ▶
1948, Nat Fein, Photograph, National Baseball Hall of Fame and Museum, Inc., Cooperstown, New York

BASE BALL

FIREMEN'S BASEBALL PARK, FRESNO, CAL.

BABE RUTH

BABE RUTH

SULTAN OF SWAT

LOU GEHRIG

WORLD'S MOST VALUABLE PLAYER

FOOTBALL

Fresno State College

vs.

St. Ignatius College

1 P. M.

At State College Stadium

LOU GEHRIG

The two teams are composed of leading Coast League and Valley Baseball Players

SATURDAY, OCT. 29

Auspices Fresno Post No. 4, American Legion

3:00 P. M.

A Ruth/Gehrig poster announcement, National Baseball Hall of Fame and Museum, Inc., Cooperstown, New York

Lou Gehrig in 1926,
Culver Pictures

LOU GEHRIG (1903–1941)

Lou Gehrig proved that nice guys do not always finish last. They can finish a glorious second. Paired, and compared, with the greatest baseball player in history, Babe Ruth, Gehrig experienced the mixed fate of fame by association with a legendary figure. He and Ruth formed the heart of the Yankees' unbeatable "Murderers' Row" of power hitters— back to back in the batting order from 1925 to 1935, Ruth third and Gehrig fourth. "Together," wrote sportswriter Joe Williams, "they formed the most destructive one–two punch baseball ever knew, the only consistent combination capable of driving in five runs with two swings, one following the other." Unquestionably, in the firm of Ruth and Gehrig, "Larrupin' Lou" was the junior partner; but it took Ruth's incredible stature to overshadow him. In baseball's holy year of 1927, when the Babe hammered out a record sixty homers, Gehrig, with him homer for homer until Ruth's final spurt, slammed in forty-seven, the greatest number to date after Ruth. Third that year was a player with only eighteen notches on his bat.

Gehrig had other close calls with batting supremacy, and a few sweet moments at the

The 1927 Yankees, considered one of the greatest teams in baseball history; Gehrig is at far left of the third row, National Baseball Hall of Fame and Museum, Inc., Cooperstown, New York

top. In the 1928 World Series, when Ruth hit .625, Gehrig chased him with a .545, highest ever for a World Series except for Ruth's. Four years later, in 1932, Gehrig bettered Ruth's series average of .333 with a stupendous .529, obscured nevertheless by the hoopla surrounding Ruth's legendary "called" homer. It was in 1932 as well, on June 3, that Gehrig had his finest day—hitting four consecutive home runs in one game. His finest year, 1934, saw him awarded the game's Triple Crown, with league-leading scores in home runs, runs batted in, and batting average. Except for his tie with Ruth in 1931, it was Gehrig's only year with the homer title.

Other players would have chafed at being baseball's eternal Crown Prince, but it was not in Gehrig's character to resent The Sultan of Swat. A modest man who once said "I'm not a headline guy," he accepted Ruth's skill and crowd-pleasing flair and even his condescension as facts of life which he never allowed to interfere with his own determination to do his best. Gehrig took quiet pride in his discipline and consistency. For thirteen straight years, he drove in more than a hundred runs. For twelve, he batted over .300. His most remarkable feat, not of physical prowess but of character, was the endurance record, which will never be equaled, of playing in 2,130 consecutive major-league games, through injuries, illness, and contract

Gehrig's farewell to baseball, July 4, 1939, United Press International

negotiations. It was for that remarkable durability above all that he was cheered on as "The Iron Horse."

The first signs of his decline caught everybody by surprise. After one year as the lone Yankee star following Ruth's retirement in 1935, and another shared with the phenomenal rookie Joe DiMaggio, Gehrig showed, at age thirty-five, a premature slowing-down of physical ability. No longer able to count on the reflexes which had made him not only a star hitter but also one of the great first basemen, he failed, for the first time since his rookie year, to average .300 and drove in no runs at the World Series. By the opening of the 1939 season, it was clear that something was seriously wrong. After making only four hits in the first eight games, "The Iron Horse" pulled in his brakes and told manager Joe McCarthy that he wanted to stop for a while. He never played again. Within a month the diagnosis was in. Gehrig was suffering from a rare illness, amyotrophic lateral sclerosis (a hardening of the spinal column), which subsequently became popularly known as "Lou Gehrig's disease." It was a death sentence which Yankees tried to soften with a day in his honor on July 4. Cheered by thousands and hugged by Ruth, Gehrig tearfully proclaimed himself "the luckiest man on the face of the earth." In two years he was dead at thirty-eight.

Bill Klem in October 1915, United Press
International

*In over forty years of umpiring, Klem had many
confrontations with managers. His nemesis, shown
here on April 16, 1940, is the feisty Leo Durocher,*
United Press International

BILL KLEM (1874–1951)

It might be said of all good umpires, but it was truest of Bill Klem: he was a man you
loved to hate. For umpires, that constitutes charisma. And Klem had it from the moment,
in 1905, when he stepped into the bottle-strewn field of the National League in baseball's
rowdiest years to his retirement from the same league in the early 1940s, when the game had
matured in its treatment of umpires to the relative refinement of mere boos and hisses.

Klem built his authority and his reputation on the rock of his perfect self-confidence.
"I never called one wrong," he often said with supreme and irritating finality; and, even
though he amended that at the end of his career to "in my heart I never did," the effect was
the same. Klem could not be moved. This brought players (honest and dishonest),
sportswriters, and managers to frenzy. The hostility reached a point where one newspaper
could headline the report of an outraged fan's fatal heart attack "Umpire Klem Kills
Innocent Fan." Klem's most consistent and powerful critic, manager John McGraw, found
that threats would not faze him. "Mr. Manager," Klem replied on one occasion, "if it's
possible for you to take my job away from me, I don't want it."

Behind the bravado was an honest sense of what baseball required of its umpires. If they
could be bullied, tricked, or undercut, the integrity of the game would collapse. When Klem
started out, a single umpire, in physical danger from fans and players, stood surveying an
entire field—where three more stand now. Subject to taunts and dodges, he might be intimidated if he could not be bought. To establish his own authority, Klem literally drew the line.
Any disruptive player was invited to cross over a mark struck in the dust by the umpire's toe,
at the risk of being tossed out of the game. Klem was as tough in insisting on the rights and

rewards of his profession. The first in baseball history to sign a three-year umpiring contract, he demanded, and received, the unprecedented sums of $650 and then $1,000 for World Series duty, in 1917 and 1918, upgrading the pay scale for his colleagues in the process.

In moments of reflection, "The Old Arbitrator," as he was called by those who learned to grow fond of him, blamed the "notoriously badly written rules of baseball" for much of the game's climate of dispute. Because they were written "by gentlemen for gentlemen"—and Klem noticed few gentlemen on the fields of his day—they were steeped in ambiguity. Until the year before Klem's death, in 1950, when the rules were rewritten, the umpire had to interpret them on the spot and stick by them. Only within the iron circle of his own conscience would Klem give in to flexibility: "In my lifetime I have seen many runners fail to touch second as they trotted around the bases after clouting the ball out of the park. When the opposing team raised the point . . . I always said, 'To me he touched second.' And to me he did, the second he hit the ball out of the park."

Klem retired, after forty years in the game, only when he doubted one of his own decisions for the first time in his career. Beloved by then—or at least grudgingly admired as an institution—he was in time honored with a special ceremony at the Polo Grounds in New York. In his speech, Klem allowed himself a rare moment of sentimentality: "Baseball is more than a game to me. It's a religion."

Game Called Because of Rain, Norman Rockwell, Oil on canvas, 1949, National Baseball Hall of Fame and Museum, Inc., Cooperstown, New York

Extending his hitting streak to forty-five games, DiMaggio passes Wee Willie Keeler's 1897 record, United Press International

JOE DiMAGGIO (b. 1914)

If Joe DiMaggio had never made those impossible game-deciding catches in center field, if he had not shown consistent, brilliant power-hitting to take the Yankees over the top time and time again, then not much attention would have been paid to the majesty of his stance and the grace of his glide. But once it was established that DiMaggio was a winner—in his historic 1936 rookie year—then the sheer joy of watching him play overtook fans, sportswriters, and fellow competitors alike. "He was," wrote Roy Blount, Jr., "the class of the Yankees in times when the Yankees outclassed everybody else." DiMaggio never played to the grandstands. No action was wasted, no opportunity lost. Out in the field, where he moved effortlessly, his catches seemed preordained. At the plate, feet well apart, bat held just off the shoulder, "The Yankee Clipper" was all flawless instinct. The pure, flowing arc of his swing described all that baseball might be. Yankee manager Casey Stengel never saw his like: "He made the rest of them look like plumbers."

DiMaggio was beautiful to see but, for two months of mounting excitement in 1941, he dominated the American imagination on yet another level. "Who started baseball's famous streak/That's set us all aglow?" went the breathless lyrics of a popular song. "Jolting Joe DiMaggio. Joe . . . Joe . . . DiMaggio." At the start, on May 15, 1941, there may have been some Americans who had never heard of "Joltin' Joe." Those who knew him were seeing a side they didn't think existed. For the ten preceding games, he had averaged only .177 in what he called "the worst slump of my life." Then the miracle happened—not overnight but

43

slowly, week by week, until people began to notice. DiMaggio was getting at least one clear hit per game. By the time Wee Willie Keeler's 1897 record of forty-four games had fallen, everyone knew something important, something *radiant,* was happening. Throughout the country, as antidote to the news of war overseas, Americans followed the DiMaggio bulletins. They might have gone on forever. DiMaggio was stopped at fifty-six games, by fate as much as anything, on July 17, but then went on to log another streak of sixteen. "Our kids will teach their kids his name," the song went on. DiMaggio's record was permanent. No one else has ever come close.

For those who followed DiMaggio's career through the ten American League pennants and nine World Series won by a team electrified by his leadership, there were many other rewards. Called "the American League's most sensational recruit since Ty Cobb," he batted in 125 runs his rookie year. Three years later, he made the catch of the century, going past the Yankee Stadium flagpole after Hank Greenberg's high fly ball to the center-field bleachers. In 1949, having suffered a crippling calcium deposit in his heel through sixty-six missed games, he returned to a career many thought was finished, and hit seven home runs in a three-game sweep against the Yankees' strongest rivals, the Boston Red Sox.

It was possible to mock Joe's look of gravity and the vanity which underlay it. Certainly he was aware of his image, and of the reverence fans brought to the experience of seeing him play. But it was, after all, a true responsibility he bore. "He knew he was Joe DiMaggio," his teammate Lefty Gomez once said, "and he knew what that meant to the country."

The Wide Swing, Harvey Dinnerstein, Oil on canvas, c. 1975, Capricorn Galleries, Bethesda, Maryland

Ted Williams, Donald Moss for Sports Illustrated, Acrylic on board, 1968, Spectrum Fine Art Gallery, New York City

TED WILLIAMS (b. 1918)

Whatever it was that made Ted Williams hit the way he did drove him hard. A cocky man dedicated to his craft, Williams shut out the world of screaming fans and critical sportswriters in pursuit of his own private standard of perfection. Nothing irritated him more than to be told that his brilliant record—six major-league batting titles, including two at ages thirty-nine and forty—was simply the result of natural talent. "You know what makes me a good hitter?" he exploded at one well-intentioned admirer. "Practice! Practice! Practice!" From his early years as a player in San Diego through two decades of power-hitting as the touchy star of the Boston Red Sox, "Tempestuous Ted" never let up on himself. Even after he achieved, in the 1941 season, the triumphant average of .406, highest in the majors since 1924, he could still brood on his limitations. "I do four out of ten jobs right," he told a friend, "and they call me a great hitter."

They called him a few other things as well. Williams's inner drive left him no energy to court the adulation of fans or even to observe the common decencies. After his rookie year, when he was last known to tip his hat to the cheering grandstands, Williams became notorious—and fascinating—for his refusal to acknowledge applause. It was, he announced, the fickleness of fans, as ready to boo as to cheer, which decided him. There were those who came to Fenway Park just for the pleasure of heckling the great hitter, and there were sportswriters, too, who made their life's work—until Williams became a municipal monument and passions cooled—the pointing-out of his deficiencies. But purists admired the cool loner in

Boston's "Tempestuous Ted," United Press International

Williams and the ideal of baseball he represented. One of them, novelist John Updike, wrote, "For me, Williams is the classic ballplayer of the game on a hot August weekday, before a small crowd, when the only thing at stake is the tissue-thin difference between a thing well done and a thing done ill."

Eventually, almost every fan in Boston came to feel Updike's awe. The Williams years were heartbreaking ones for the Red Sox—only one pennant and several end-of-the-season near-misses—but Ted's strong left arm upheld Boston's pride. There was the classic moment in the 1941 All-Star game when, in the last of the ninth inning—two on base, two outs, two strikes—Williams hit a home run to hand the American League a 7–5 victory—so unexpected that the game's announcer, the great Red Barber, was rendered speechless.

And there were the comebacks: after his hero's duty in the Korean War, he played the last thirty-seven games of the 1953 season and, in ninety-one times at the plate, connected thirty-seven times, including thirteen home runs. And, after a two-and-a-half-month absence to heal a broken shoulder, he jumped into a double-header and hit eight out of nine times at bat, two of them homers. That was enough to dull resentment in all but the most belligerent fans. In time, "Tempestuous Ted" became "Our Teddy" and the most admired sports figure in Boston. When, in 1960, Williams hit his last homer, number 521, the longest of his career, the stands at Fenway exploded with pride and affection. He left the field without tipping his hat—his own man to the last.

SATCHEL PAIGE (b. 1906?)

The reputation of a great athlete is made in the few years given him when his body is finely honed and his spirit triumphant. For most, the period goes all too fast. But, for one Leroy "Satchel" Paige, the time of greatness stretched, incredibly, over three decades. From his early years, pitching for the segregated black leagues during the 1920s, to the breakthrough moment when he was signed for the major leagues in the late 1940s, and beyond, Paige was a certifiable sports phenomenon. Not a few baseball writers, looking over Paige's performance in his first year with the Cleveland Indians at age forty-two (or more; his age has never been pinned down), seriously suggested that he be named Rookie of the Year. "I declined the position," Paige wryly responded. "I wasn't sure which year the gentlemen had in mind." Nearly two decades later, when he was somewhere near fifty-nine and out of full service in the majors, he was still capable of pitching three scoreless innings for the Kansas City Athletics. For Satchel Paige, youth never seemed to end.

No one will ever know whether Paige was the greatest pitcher ever. Performing his wonders in the statistical morass of sandlot, semi-pro, and exhibition baseball for so many years, he was never charted for the record books. But one only had to see him or hear about him to imagine what might have happened had his race not barred him from the majors. Once, in 1933, he had a winning stretch of twenty-one *consecutive* games and sixty-two scoreless innings. They say that he pitched about a hundred no-hitters and that he won 2,000 of roughly 2,500 games. Competition in the majors might well have been tougher (although certain men he went against in the black leagues, like long-distance hitter Josh Gibson, would have given Joe DiMaggio a run for his money), but then Satch would, at least, have been allowed some rest between games. His playing schedule was relentless. There were weeks on end when he pitched daily, and twice on Saturday and Sunday. And yet he won and won again. When he did get his licks in against major-league talent in exhibition games, he proved that he was up to the best of them. Once, Dizzy Dean went against him in a contest that lasted for thirteen innings, and lost, 1–0. In 1947, in the game that convinced Cleveland Indians owner Bill Veeck to take him on the next year, Paige defeated ace pitcher Bob Feller, 8–0, and struck out sixteen batters in the process.

Satch may have pitched for more than 250 teams before he joined the Indians. He worked with the best black teams—the Birmingham Black Barons, the Pittsburgh Crawfords, the Kansas City Monarchs—but, for years on end, he also barnstormed as a solo star anywhere in the United States and in the Caribbean, for one day, one week, or longer: "Satchel Paige, world's greatest pitcher, guaranteed to strike out the first nine men." It was grueling, but he could make up to $35,000 a year, and he became a legend. His first appearance on the mound in Cleveland brought a ten-minute foot-stomping ovation from major-league fans eager to see for themselves such Paige specialities as a slowball he called the "barber," or the "two-hump blooper," guaranteed to graze the batter's chin, or the fastball "Long Tom," or the hesitation pitch, which he stopped in mid-throw.

Paige stayed with Cleveland until 1950, and then went to the St. Louis Browns for three years and had the satisfaction of being selected by Casey Stengel for the American League All-Star team of 1952. He rounded off his career as he had started it, barnstorming with some of his old teams, never quite giving up the game he was born to play. In 1968, at sixty-two, he put on the uniform of the Atlanta Braves for the 158 days he needed to qualify for a pension. Major-league baseball owed him that—and much more.

Satchel Paige, National Baseball Hall of Fame and Museum, Inc., Cooperstown, New York

Paige welcomes Jackie Robinson to the Kansas City Monarchs. Within a few years the scene would be reversed,
as Robinson welcomed Paige to the major leagues, Jackie Robinson Foundation, Brooklyn

A young Jackie Robinson,
Jackie Robinson Foundation,
Brooklyn

JACKIE ROBINSON (1919–1972)

Had Jackie Robinson rested on his laurels as the first black player to be signed for the major leagues, he would have become no more than an inspiring footnote in the history of baseball. Instead, he is remembered as one of the strongest competitors the game has ever known. It did not take many months after he had joined the Brooklyn Dodgers in 1947 for even the race-obsessed in the Ebbets Field grandstands to forget the integration hullabaloo in the fascination of watching a heroic athlete dominate the field.

Robinson had had many years to prepare for the opportunity which might never have come. Raised in Southern California, he excelled in every sport he attempted during high school and several years at the University of California at Los Angeles, and might have made a career of either football or basketball given the chance. After three years in the Army and a brief stint as a coach in Austin, Texas, he signed on with the Kansas City Monarchs of the Negro American League in 1945 and made a sensational debut as a shortstop. That year, at twenty-six, he was approached by Branch Rickey, part-owner and general manager of the Brooklyn Dodgers, to take his place in history. Robinson, who agreed to the difficult condition that he not fight even when provoked, was sent as far north as the Dodger farm-

49

Robinson renews his contract in 1949 with Dodger owner Branch Rickey, the man responsible for bringing blacks into the major leagues, Jackie Robinson Foundation, Brooklyn

The Brooklyn Dodgers, 1947, Jackie Robinson Foundation, Brooklyn

club system could take him to test the waters in Montreal. He found them warm and welcoming. Robinson's year with the Canadian team ended with a triumphant "Little World Series" against Louisville. So overwhelming was the fans' reaction that he was chased down the street outside the stadium until a passing car rescued him. "It's probably the first time a white mob of rioters ever chased a Negro down the street in love rather than hate," wrote a visiting reporter from Louisville.

Robinson joined the Dodgers the following year, and faced an ugly period of racial taunts from some of his fellow players, and even anonymous threats on his life, before he settled the matter that he was in the game to stay. He did it by providing a smarter reason than his color to fear Jackie Robinson. Always willing to take a chance, alert to exploit even the slightest slips and misjudgments, "Robbie" put a whole generation of opponents on edge. For ten years, Brooklyn fans, savoring six pennants and one world championship, had stories to swap about Robinson stealing home—he did it an incredible nineteen times—or faking bunts and steals, driving the pitchers wild with distraction. That first difficult season, when the Dodgers management doubled the pressure already on him by testing him in every position but pitcher and catcher, Robinson's combative spirit carried him to his selection as Rookie of the Year. Two seasons later—in command of his best position, second base— Robinson took the Most Valuable Player award, won the major-league batting championship, and led the league in stolen bases.

In 1951 anyone left in America who doubted the powerful role that blacks would play in major-league baseball was silenced by the most dramatic pennant race in memory, between the Giants, propelled by Willie Mays, and the Dodgers, kept alive by Jackie Robinson. The final Dodgers game of the regular season, a showcase for Robbie's talents, went fourteen innings against the Phillies and was saved for Brooklyn when, in the twelfth, Robinson made a stunning catch of a near-tie-breaking line drive and then, in the fourteenth, hit the winning home run, forcing the Giants to a play-off. It was hard to believe that anyone had ever wondered if Jackie Robinson should be allowed to play major-league ball.

Robinson stealing home in a game against the Philadelphia Phillies, 1950, Wide World Photos, Inc.

Willie Mays at bat,
Fred Kaplan, Photo-
graph, Collection of
the photographer

52

Mays's cheerful spirit became his trademark, Hy Peskin, Photograph, 1962, Sports Illustrated

Below:
Mays won the Most Valuable Player award in 1954 and 1965, Willie Mays

WILLIE MAYS (b. 1931)

There must have been times when Willie Mays did not want to go out on that field. But he never let the fans know. Any opportunity to see him play—all dash and sparkle—was a guarantee of pleasure. Mays's buoyant spirit reminded everyone, whether or not he rooted for the Giants, that major-league baseball began as a game remembered from childhood. "He brought to the game," wrote sportswriter Roger Kahn, "the deepest enthusiasm to play I've ever seen. He was the ultimate combination of the professional full of talent and the amateur, a word that traces to the Latin *amator,* lover: and suggests one who brings a passion to what he does." The sportswriters liked to say that the highly paid star would have played for free and, even though he denied that, he knew and appreciated what they meant.

People expected wonders from Mays: the special plays of which only he seemed capable. His virtuosity might be expressed in a trademark "basket catch" of fly balls, hands nonchalantly cupped by his waist; or in a sudden dash out from under his hat and into the stolen base; or in a torrent of home runs—four during one incredible game on the road in

1961. "Willie is without doubt," exulted Giants manager Leo Durocher, "the most dynamic, most dramatic, most fantastic, most exciting performer in action today. He is Joe Louis, Jascha Heifetz, Sammy Davis, and Nashua rolled into one."

Mays spent more years playing for the Giants in San Francisco than in New York, but his mystique was forged in those first golden years at the Polo Grounds. Nurtured by Leo Durocher during his initial crisis of confidence, Mays exploded, later in 1951, with a force that carried the Giants from hopelessness, six weeks before season's end, to a historic play-off and pennant victory. Mays, with his "say hey" greeting for everyone, was the miracle man of baseball. Those who doubted had only to see what happened to the team during its two-season slump while the "say hey" kid was away in the Army from 1952 to 1953. When he returned in 1954, so did the magic. The Giants took the pennant that year and a four-game sweep of the World Series with the Cleveland Indians. The last disbeliever was converted during the game that broke the Indians' back, when Willie caught Vic Wertz's 450-foot drive after it sailed over his head, and then managed—no one could imagine how—to spin around and get a perfect throw back to the infield before sprawling.

Mays had his off-days and even his off-years but, over the course of a career from twenty-year-old Giants rookie to dean of baseball players at forty-two, he showed consistent drive and talent. Chosen Most Valuable Player in 1954, he had in time another season so good that he was anointed Most Valuable Player again a full eleven years later. Even with nearly two seasons of peak batting power lost to the Army, Mays slammed in 660 home runs, chasing Babe Ruth's record. But what lingered in the memory longest was his sense of drama. Traded to the Mets twenty years after his start in New York with the Giants, the veteran celebrated his emotional first game back in that city—against the San Francisco Giants—with a tie-breaking home run. Above all players, he understood and delivered the symbolic moment.

Mays stealing third against the Brooklyn Dodgers, Ebbets Field, Robert Riger,
Photograph, 1955, Collection of the photographer

In the 1954 World Series, Mays made a game-saving catch of Clevelander Vic Wertz's 450-foot drive ball at the base of centerfield wall, Wide World Photos, Inc.

Casey Stengel,
Rhoda Sherbell,
Polychromed bronze, 1965,
National Portrait Gallery,
Smithsonian Institution

Stengel, happy after a win against Cleveland, June 6, 1959, Wide World Photos, Inc.

CASEY STENGEL (1889–1975)

As far back as his earliest years in baseball, Casey Stengel was an inspired clown. Able enough as a player on such big-league teams as the Dodgers and the Giants, young Stengel, not yet rubber-faced, made himself memorable to the fans through his mugging, his pranks, and one immortal gesture—when he tipped his cap to a hostile crowd and released a trapped sparrow. That was style, but was it baseball? The sportswriters had to take him seriously in a historic World Series (1923) when Stengel hit, in separate games, the first two World Series home runs in the new Yankee Stadium, both game-winning. But even then, at his moment of triumph, there was something comic about Casey lumbering around the bases, "his flanks heaving," to hear Damon Runyon report it, "his breath whistling, his head far back."

Yet everyone knew that the clown was no fool. He had a first-rate baseball mind, which was put to use in 1926, at the end of his career as a player, when he received the first of a lifetime string of managing assignments. Twenty-three years later, riding high with the first of many Yankee pennants, Stengel would become famous as a man who loved baseball, but this was the time when he proved it. Over two decades, marked for the most part by bad teams and bad luck, Stengel worked his way out of the minors only to face bleak years in the major leagues, including stints with the Dodgers and the Boston Braves. For one nine-year stretch, he never managed to break out of second division. Then it was back to the minors— Milwaukee, Kansas City, and Oakland.

The sportswriters had him pegged until George Weiss, general manager of the Yankees, reached down into the minors and picked Stengel to manage his flagging team. The wisdom went that Stengel could only have been chosen to mug for the fans a couple of years while Weiss searched around for a real manager. In fact he had found one already—perhaps the greatest in baseball history. In his incredible first year, 1949, Stengel pushed a team riddled with injuries to a pennant on the last day of the season. For twelve historic years, the old man rode the Yankees to ten pennants—five at one stretch, for a record—and seven world championships. He had the talent—DiMaggio, Yogi Berra, Mickey Mantle, Whitey Ford— and he knew what to do with it. Old Case, magician of the lineup, invented the two-platoon system, sending left-handed hitters against right-handed pitchers, and an army of right-handers against southpaws. To search out young talent, he inaugurated preseason tryout camps for minor-league prospects—and one of them turned out to be Mickey Mantle.

But no one ever called Stengel a mere technician. He was the joy of baseball incarnate, a screwy monologist with the habit of tripping over his own syntax who somehow managed to express all the seriousness and all the craziness of the national game. Always surrounded by a loving press corps, he was photographed in every imaginable position and quoted on every imaginable subject. After the Yankee management unceremoniously fired him in 1960, for reasons of age, he carried the nation's affection with him when he took on another job of managing, in 1962, the upstart National League franchise, the New York Mets. His love affair with the fans made the perennial losers a top attraction. When Stengel retired in 1967, he attained the closest thing to athletic sainthood. "I want to thank all my players," he once said in purest Stengelese, "for giving me the honor of being what I was."

Stengel and his triumphant New York Yankees, October 2, 1949, after defeating the Boston Red Sox to win the American League pennant, Wide World Photos, Inc.

Mickey Mantle, James Drake, Photograph, 1965,
Sports Illustrated

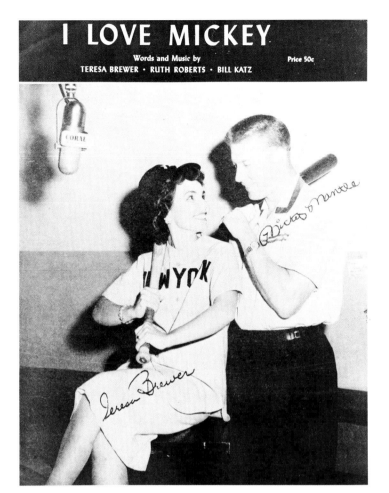

*Mantle's popular appeal earned him a song, in the tradition of
"King" Kelly and Babe Ruth,* National Baseball Hall of Fame and
Museum, Inc., Cooperstown, New York

MICKEY MANTLE (b. 1931)

By the early 1950s, Yankee fans had grown quite used to having a royal line of hitters who
roused the team and cheered the nation. Ruth and Gehrig had started it all. DiMaggio had
kept the magic going. Now another generation confidently awaited its own hero. Nineteen-
year-old Mickey Mantle, fresh from the West and a near-miss from the life of a coal miner,
found himself the anointed prince of the Yankee dynasty. Powerfully built and fast on his
feet, Mantle received a monumental buildup before his rookie 1951 season which left no
room for error. When the errors came, the young slugger, crushed by his poor showing and
harassed by the hostility of disappointed fans, was returned to the minor leagues in mid-
season. In a month he was back.

The fans had been right the first time. Mantle became the next Yankee miracle. Given
the time he needed to develop, the switch-hitter provided thrills worthy of the old masters.
In 1953 he caused a sensation in Washington's Griffith Stadium by sending a ball over
the left-field wall, to land in a back yard some 565 feet from home plate. After that the
tape measures were always ready when Mantle was up. By the middle of the decade, he came
far closer than anyone before to sending a homer outside Yankee Stadium. The ball, heading
toward the right-field roof, just missed clearing the facade at the edge. In 1961, ten years
after that first miserable season, he and roommate Roger Maris engaged in the most

59

spectacular home-run race in baseball history to break Babe Ruth's record of a sixty-home-run season, set thirty-four years before. Maris, with sixty-one, took the Most Valuable Player award that year. But Mantle could afford to be generous. He had taken it in 1956 and 1957. In 1962 he would become a three-time winner.

Mantle's body was perfectly built for baseball—above the waist. Described by one writer as "the bull-necked broad-backed blond with the bric-a-brac legs," he carried the burden of an incredible assortment of disabilities. Suffering osteomyelitis in his left ankle and arthritis in his right knee, he went through a series of muscle pulls and operations, winning-season after winning-season. His manager, Casey Stengel, called him "the best one-legged player I ever saw." Mantle managed to keep going through a bandaging ritual that became as legendary as his hitting. Each day, before a game, he arrived in the locker room early enough to tightly bind his right leg from shin to thigh—giving support to his bad knee and vulnerable hamstring muscle. Then Mantle was ready to play and play hard. Those "bric-a-brac legs" carried him through twelve pennant victories.

No one ever called Mickey Mantle a happy player. Too much pain and frustration had gone into the shaping of his career. But he was a determined one. "He'd minimize his injuries to get to play," remembered the doctor who had seen him through operations on both knees, a hip, and a shoulder. "He's the kind of guy you'd like to have in your outfit in war." What kept Mantle going was the memory of a father who had pushed him hard to demand everything of himself. While the world admired his power and his courage, Mantle raged against his imperfections. "He got mad at himself, but not at anyone else," remembered teammate Jerry Coleman. "When he failed to get a hit, or struck out, he would come into the dugout and with his fist would hit the water cooler. There wasn't a water cooler in the league that Mantle didn't hit." That anger and determination pushed him on through 2,401 games in eighteen seasons crowned by 536 home runs. As a two-legged player, he might have closed the record books.

Mantle getting a hero's welcome from fans after hitting a home run in 1959,
Wide World Photos, Inc.

Mantle played throughout his career with his right leg heavily bandaged,
Hy Peskin, Photograph, 1956, Sports Illustrated

SANDY KOUFAX (b. 1935)

Sandy Koufax's twelve-year record in the major leagues split right down the middle—half famine, half feast. Recruited by the Dodgers out of the sandlots of Brooklyn, the young left-handed pitcher went through six relentless seasons of disappointment. No one doubted Koufax's talent. The power behind his fastball promised greatness. Only rarely, however, did he deliver on that promise. One day in the Los Angeles Coliseum, he electrified the crowd with eighteen strikeouts. During the World Series of 1959, he turned in a stellar performance. But overall the record was grim: thirty-six victories and forty defeats from 1955 to 1960. That last year the Dodgers cut his salary.

Koufax had what it took, but he lacked control. Catcher Norm Sherry, facing another barrage of wild bullets from the pitcher's mound, persuaded his friend, during spring training of 1961, to loosen up and to vary his technique. "Then and there," Koufax later recalled, "I realized that there's no need to throw as hard as I can. I found that if I take it easy and throw naturally, the ball goes just as fast." In charge now of his fastball and of a new curve ball that catcher John Roseboro said "collapses at the plate like a folding chair," Koufax was on his way. In that turnaround year, he logged eighteen wins to thirteen losses and struck out 269 batters, breaking the league record held by the greatest pitcher to date, Christy Mathewson.

From 1961 to 1966, Koufax's star rose with the speed of his fastball. He was a certified phenomenon. Four years he led the league in strikeouts, three years in victories. His last year, he led everyone in everything—victories, innings played, strikeouts, shutouts, complete games. But the artist in Koufax found greatest satisfaction in the four no-hitters he pitched in four successive seasons. The first inning of the first game, against the New York Mets, on May 30, 1962, was the finest of his career: three strikeouts in nine pitches. The last no-hitter, against the Chicago Cubs in September of 1965, was a perfect game: twenty-seven batters up, twenty-seven batters down, no hits, no walks, no errors.

The fans came to expect miracles of Koufax but, even on his off-days, they were fascinated by his intensity. Warming up, getting his abused pitching muscles in shape, he seemed to push and stretch himself into postures the human body was never meant to take. His stance on the mound was not graceful—he could, in fact, look grotesque—but there was beauty in his perfect concentration of body and spirit.

Koufax's brooding nature impressed the legions of sportswriters assigned to cover him. He seemed, wrote one, to realize at the very height of his glory "that none of it can last." The first hint of his professional mortality came in 1962 when he developed a circulation problem, but it was in 1964, with the discovery of traumatic arthritis in his pitching elbow, that his future as a player became uncertain. As the pain persisted, Sandy took on the aspect of a tragic hero. The fans knew the price of his brilliant pitching—the cortisone shots and the buckets of ice bathing his crooked elbow after a full nine innings of torture. They saw him win, too, time and time again, and wondered how long it could last, how long he could stand it. His decision to quit, after a brilliant 1966 season, came as no surprise. "I didn't want to take the chance of disabling myself," he told reporters. "I don't regret for one minute the twelve years I've spent in baseball but I could regret one season too many." One hundred twenty-nine games won and only forty-seven lost during his six triumphant years, Koufax left baseball a satisfied man. Five years later he was elected to the Baseball Hall of Fame, the youngest veteran ever.

◀ *Sandy Koufax in action,* Neil Leifer, Photograph, 1965, Sports Illustrated

ROBERTO CLEMENTE (1934–1972)

Roberto Clemente did not belong to the "aw shucks" school of soft-spoken athletes. He knew that he was great—one of the finest baseball players ever; and he knew that he was not supposed to say it. But he did, often, and the sportswriters had him on a platter. Clemente was arrogant, they claimed; he lacked perspective. What too many of them forgot to notice, over years of his consistently brilliant playing—until Clemente's awesome performance for the Pittsburgh Pirates in the 1971 World Series converted the last disbeliever—was that the Puerto Rican champion was absolutely right.

The great publicity machine of modern baseball is always in search of superstars—but on its own terms. Easygoing Willie Mays fit the bill. Intense, brooding Roberto Clemente did not. For one thing, he was not a power hitter, preferring line drives which did the job over the theatricality of the home run. But he was, like Mays, a total player, capable of brilliant hitting and running, and heart-stopping fielding. If the nation was slow to realize what Pittsburgh and Puerto Rico had known from the start about Clemente's superiority, it was in large part because his temperament mystified the sportswriters. Clemente was not afraid to show his feelings. When he was angry or resentful, he unburdened himself to the lockerroom press; when he was battered, he announced it; when he was triumphant, he exulted. Labeled a complainer and even a malingerer—although few since Ty Cobb drove themselves harder—he claimed to be misunderstood, and was.

Clemente, in his own words, "played mad all the time." But then things began to change. In 1966, eleven years after starting with the Pirates, he was chosen Most Valuable Player of the National League. The following year, a meeting of general managers of the major-league teams, convened in Mexico City, surprised itself by picking the Puerto Rican star as the best player in both leagues, a "one-man team." But complete vindication awaited the World Series, Pirates against Baltimore Orioles, in 1971. Roger Angell, poet among baseball observers, wrote that Clemente played "a kind of baseball that none of us had ever seen before—throwing and running and hitting at something close to the level of perfection." His flawless right-fielding, his leadership, his twelve hits adding up to a .414 Series average, made Clemente—at last—a household name.

Clemente's years in baseball, never lacking for drama, ended on a triumphant note. His last regular-season hit—of his career, and of his life—was his three-thousandth, on September 29, 1972. Three months later, he was dead, at thirty-eight, in a plane crash during a flight to help victims of the Nicaraguan earthquake. Folk hero and now martyr in Puerto Rico, he was mourned as few athletes have been. Clemente had begun his life in baseball determined to provide his countrymen with a hero like Babe Ruth—to be "the best there was . . . a Puerto Rican player they could say that about, someone to look up to and try to equal." That need was the engine of his spirit. And the sportswriters finally understood.

A proud Roberto Clemente, 1972,
United Press International

Clemente strikes out, Tony Triolo,
Photograph, 1970, Sports Illustrated

Hank Aaron after hitting his 715th homer and passing Babe Ruth's record, Neil Leifer, Photograph, 1974, Sports Illustrated

HANK AARON (b. 1934)

The baseball establishment was forever "discovering" Hank Aaron. In 1957, when Aaron hit the homer in the eleventh inning (and the eleventh hour) which clinched the pennant for the Milwaukee Braves, he was hailed as a new star and, after a brilliant World Series, chosen the National League's Most Valuable Player. Years of power-hitting later—in Milwaukee and then Atlanta for the Braves—Aaron again surfaced in the headlines during his banner year of 1970, when he became only the eighth player, the youngest since Ty Cobb, to log three thousand hits, and the first of the eight also to pound out five hundred homers. "For sixteen years," Aaron said with understandable irritation, "no one knew I was playing baseball. Then suddenly everybody began to wonder where I came from." It happened again three seasons later when Hank collected his seven-hundredth homer and began the countdown to overtake Babe Ruth's magical 714. One writer noted, typically, that Aaron had for years "been sneaking up, as it were, on the record."

How a home-run king could swing hard for nearly two decades with only scant notice in the national press is one of the mysteries of publicity. In part it was a matter of geography. Milwaukee and Atlanta could not provide the limelight as easily as New York and Los Angeles. Then there was Aaron's unflamboyant style. Overshadowed by Mickey Mantle and Willie Mays, he played a solid, undramatic game. With the air of a businessman making his rounds, Hank traveled the bases coolly, his face a mask. After the shining 1957 homer which decided the pennant, he announced, "I'm excited for the first time in my life."

But writers and fans were wrong to conclude that the impassive Aaron failed to give his all: "Just because I don't jump and holler . . . doesn't mean that I don't go all out. Maybe I don't look like I'm hustling, but that's just my way."

Aaron's patience got him through. Year after year he produced, writing his name all over the record books. Becoming second only to Ty Cobb in career hits, he would one day be first in runs batted in, first in bases, first in extra base hits, first in times at bat, first in games played. But the "first" that mattered, the one that brought Aaron the applause so long denied him, was the home-run title everyone had assumed was forever Babe Ruth's.

To those protective of the Babe's memory, it was a matter of the tortoise overtaking the hare. Ruth had scored his record in over 2,800 fewer times at bat. But the spoilers were drowned out by a national cheering section as Aaron ended his twentieth season a few homers short of immortality. The Aaron-watch paid off on April 8, 1974, when the largest crowd ever to watch a game in the Atlanta stadium saw Hank slam homer number 715 off Al Downing of the Los Angeles Dodgers. Overwhelmed by a sea of autographed Babe Ruth baseballs, Aaron signed them all, content to share his glory with the demigod whose name would always be linked with his. And he was not through yet. By the time he retired in 1976 after two additional seasons as a designated hitter with the Milwaukee Brewers, the forty-two-year-old slugger with the whiplash swing made 755 career homers the record to beat. That was a number baseball would never forget.

Aaron caught off third base in a game between the Los Angeles Dodgers and the Milwaukee Braves, 1965, United Press International

Stag at Sharkey's, George Bellows, Oil on canvas, 1907, Cleveland Museum of Art, Hinman B. Hurlbut Collection

BOXING

Biography by
MARC PACHTER

Boxer, Samuel Murray, Bronze, 1899,
Yale University Art Gallery, Whitney Collection of Sporting Art

Between Rounds, Thomas Eakins, Oil on canvas, 1899, ▶
Philadelphia Museum of Art

John L. Sullivan,
J. M. Mora, Photo-
graph, 1882, Library
of Congress

Sullivan championship banner, 1882, The National Museum of American History, Smithsonian Institution

JOHN L. SULLIVAN (1858-1918)

During the ten years of his manly glory—from the day in 1882 when he pounded Paddy Ryan into submission in Mississippi City, to the historic bout with Gentleman Jim Corbett a decade later, when he paid the price for too much good living—John L. Sullivan, "The Boston Strong Boy," ruled his brawling age. Man's man, ladies' man, hero to boys, and inspiration to poets, "The Great John L." was a phenomenon of near-universal appeal, America's first, and perhaps greatest, national sports idol. "Let Me Shake the Hand That Shook the Hand of Sullivan," went a popular song, and those inclined to more robust worship might have a go at the John L. Sullivan Punching Machine—"How Hard Can You Hit the Great John L.?" He seemed invincible; he *was* magnificent, mustachioed, barrel-chested, and strong as an ox.

Like his fighting style, Sullivan's personality was basic. His appetites were huge, and he satisfied them on a heroic scale—six quarts of whiskey went down his throat on one celebrated occasion. There was no pretension to him, no restraint. A bruiser with little interest in the niceties of the law, he practiced his bare-knuckled trade at the time when it was banned in all thirty-eight states. Sullivan was *game*—he would fight anyone anywhere, on a barge in the Hudson, in the Mississippi backwoods, or as a professor of pugilism giving exhibition matches in the local opera house. It was hard not to love him.

One man who did resist his charm, Richard Kyle Fox, owner of the *Police Gazette,* promoted his hatred of the Boston Strong Boy into a match which ended the bare-knuckle era. Seeking vengeance for a supposed snub, Fox found a worthy pugilist in Jake Kilrain, pronounced him the truer champion, and sealed the investiture by presenting him with a diamond-studded belt. The aggrieved populace of Boston bestowed upon their beloved John L. a grander belt, with 397 diamonds, and urged him on. The fight, when it came, was brutal. In a secret site on the estate of a Mississippi sportsman, Sullivan and Kilrain went at each other for seventy-five rounds of slugging and wrestling (allowed under the London Prize Ring rules). Two hours and sixteen minutes after the first punch, Kilrain's corner threw in the sponge for fear that their man would die of exhaustion. Kilrain lived to be a pallbearer at Sullivan's funeral in 1918, but he had met his match. The Great John L. was unbeatable.

To the best of the bare-knuckle champions belongs the credit for changing the rules of the American ring. Tired of dodging the authorities—the governor of Mississippi had him extradited from New York to pay a one-thousand-dollar fine for the Kilrain fight—Sullivan switched to the Marquis of Queensberry rules of three-minute rounds and padded gloves ("pillows," the traditionalists hooted). Unwittingly he had ushered in the era of the ring scientist, personified by Gentleman Jim Corbett. The battle between them in New Orleans was an embarrassing rout. When Sullivan panted his concession of defeat, his fans blinked in disbelief, and saw the end of their age. The defeated champion, who still had many good years left as a star of the melodramatic stage, took it all very well. "My friends," he announced, "I have fought once too often. But if I had to get licked, I'm glad it was by an American! Yours truly, John L. Sullivan."

Introducing John L. Sullivan: *In boxing's traditional gesture of respect toward former champions, the aging Sullivan is introduced to cheering crowds before the main event,* George Bellows, Lithograph, 1916, National Portrait Gallery, Smithsonian Institution

James J. Corbett, Champion of the World, Strobridge
Lithograph Company, after a photograph by Morrison,
Lithograph, c. 1895, Chicago Historical Society

Corbett (right) *defending his title against*
British champion Charlie Mitchell in 1894.
The bout was actually fought with gloves,
Giles & Co. lithograph, 1893,
Chicago Historical Society

JAMES J. CORBETT (1866–1933)

James J. Corbett's challenge was supposed to be a joke, a bid by a presumptuous California
dandy—gutsy enough, with a decided flair in his jabs and footwork, but hardly the man to
take on John L. Sullivan. Lithe and trim beside Sullivan's powerful beefiness, a high dresser
in a world of knockabouts, Corbett fed his opponent's overconfidence.

  Sullivan first paraded his contempt for the young challenger by agreeing to an exhibition bout in San Francisco only on condition that the match be conducted in dress clothes. He sneered, too, when he pronounced Corbett a poor third choice as contender for the first heavyweight championship to be fought under the Marquis of Queensberry rules. But Corbett showed himself capable of his own brand of bravado. Before the fight of the century, held in New Orleans on September 7, 1892, he coolly announced, "I can lick him without getting my hair mussed." He did.

Corbett's sleek elegance belied his thorough grounding in the rough-and-tumble school of late-nineteenth-century boxing. Born to the shady side of the lower middle class in one of San Francisco's tough Irish neighborhoods, he developed early the knack of throwing his opponent off guard. Dressed to the hilt, the young bank clerk would enter the netherworld of the Barbary Coast to wipe the smiles off the faces of hooting barflies. He earned the right to take on Sullivan by enduring a grueling series of bouts with his Bay Area rival, Joe Choynski, and then going on, after a noteworthy victory over Sullivan's old nemesis, Jake Kilrain, to take on the splendid black Australian boxer, Peter Jackson, for a sixty-one-round draw.

Gentleman Jim was a strategist of boxing, a collector of jabs, feints, hooks, and other ring refinements which he would call upon to torment and bewilder his opponents. He was a master of timing and a genius at fancy footwork; and no one could equal him as a practical psychologist. Corbett added mind to brawn and made the guardians of respectability respectful. Because of him, American boxing became a broad-based spectator sport rather than an organized brawl.

And he reaped the rewards. Although Sullivan enjoyed success outside the ring on the vaudeville and melodrama circuits, Corbett was the first sports hero to be fully commercialized. Classically handsome and a fair actor as well, he toured for three years in a thinly disguised vehicle for his celebrityhood, the melodrama *Gentleman Jack*. The triumphant fifth act offered a rousing, orchestrated "championship fight" which never failed to bring the theater audience to its feet. The more worshipful of them could carry home a plaster-cast paperweight of the hand that had leveled the Great John L.

Corbett's vogue did not last beyond his defeat as heavyweight champion in 1897. Ironically, it was an unsophisticated fighter, Bob Fitzsimmons, who avenged John L. by bringing Corbett down with the first "solar plexus" blow. But Corbett's influence continued —as a model for all future fighters of what boxing at its most elegant could be.

Jack Johnson in 1910, Bill
Cayton, The Big Fights, Inc.

JACK JOHNSON (1878–1946)

Had the first black man to win the heavyweight championship of the world been less powerful as a boxer and a personality, the white-controlled boxing world might have been able to forgive his triumph. But Jack Johnson was not one to pander to the sensibilities of threatened Caucasians. A tough, arrogant giant of a man out of Galveston, Texas, he accused the white heavyweight champions of cowering behind the color line until, in 1908, one of them, Tommy Burns, stepped out long enough to be flattened by him into humility.

The resulting hysteria brought boxing to its lowest point. In the charged racial climate of the time, the defeat of an outclassed champion constituted nothing less than a challenge to the survival of the white race. A call went out for anyone who could, wrote one Omaha sportswriter, "restore to the Caucasians the crown of elemental greatness as measured by strength of blow, power of heart and being." Novelist and sportsman Jack London begged ex-champion Jim Jeffries to "remove the golden smile from Jack Johnson's face." Two years later, Johnson's famous smile was even broader, as Jeffries went down in the Tex Rickard–promoted carnival, on July 4, 1910, in Reno. A shock wave swept the country and sent a fantastic succession of "white hopes" into battle with each other for the privilege of defending the honor of their kind.

The boxing public was more than afraid of Johnson; they were infuriated by him. His effortless mastery in the ring allowed him to assume a cocky disregard for the seriousness of the occasion. He often engaged in light banter, not only with his puffing opponent but with the fans in the front rows, and one time, during the fateful Jeffries fight, he held up his pants with an American flag for a belt. Johnson was master of the art of enjoying himself inside and outside the ring. His appetite for luxury was huge, and he denied himself very little. Only in boxing did he play by the rules, and then only sometimes. In his private life—and there was very little private about it—he flouted the code against interracial marriage three times in succession.

Only when he was convicted of a violation of the Mann Act (under circumstances which suggest a conspiracy against him) did he find himself cornered. Unwilling to face prison, he forfeited his bail and the posh Café de Champion he owned in Chicago, and went into adventurous exile in Europe as a vaudeville star. When, in 1915, the epic search for a white knight turned up a backwoods giant, Jess Willard, Johnson agreed to meet him as close to the United States as he could safely get, in Havana, Cuba. Johnson later said that he had taken a dive in the twenty-sixth in return for a guarantee of immunity from prosecution in the United States, but more likely the years of good living had sapped his strength. In any case, he took defeat in stride and a year in Leavenworth Prison, too, when he finally returned from exile in 1920.

Johnson's fabulous life rolled on. One moment he was on the inspirational-lecture circuit (in 1924 he addressed a klavern of the Ku Klux Klan on sportsmanship); the next he was playing the Ethiopian general in the New York production of *Aida*. He died in 1946, in the last of a series of auto accidents which friends alarmed at his fast driving had known would one day take his life.

Johnson had lived long enough to see the second black heavyweight champion, Joe Louis, rule the roost. "Jack Johnson struck a double blow when he became heavyweight champion," announced his eulogist. "If we hadn't had a Jack, we wouldn't have a Joe now."

Johnson, probably in 1912, Samuel A. Marrs,
Photograph, Chicago Historical Society

Johnson with his second wife, Etta Duryea, A. Chickering,
Photograph, 1910, Library of Congress

Johnson's victory over Jim Jeffries in 1910 sent shock waves through the boxing world and led to a call for a "White Hope" to defeat him, Bill Cayton, The Big Fights, Inc.

Jess Willard KO's Johnson in the twenty-sixth round. Boxing enthusiasts still dispute whether Johnson took a deliberate dive, National Portrait Gallery, Smithsonian Institution

Below:
A young Jack Dempsey,
Ring Boxing Hall of Fame, New York

Opposite:
Through the Ropes: *Even though Firpo
knocked him out of the ring, Dempsey
came back to win the fight,* George Bellows,
Oil on canvas, 1924, Whitney Museum
of American Art, New York

JACK DEMPSEY (b. 1895)

If ever a man gave brutality a good name, it was Jack Dempsey, heavyweight champion of the world from 1919 to 1926. In boxing's long history of gentleman pugilists and barroom brawlers, scientific fighters and slashing brutes, Dempsey stood alone, villain and hero both. He was "The Idol," and "The Manassa Mauler," and just plain "Killer," and no one among the more than five hundred thousand fans who saw him in action during his heyday was able to take his eyes off him.

Jess Willard, Dempsey's first victim in a series of epic heavyweight bouts, never knew what hit him. Cocksure, he had infuriated Dempsey's manager, "Doc" Kearns, by asking for legal immunity in case he killed the challenger. A smaller man who wouldn't let up, Dempsey was always on the offensive, bobbing, crouching, pounding away: an avenging angel hypnotized by his own ferocity. By fight's end, "The Pottawatomie Giant," 250 pounds to Dempsey's 189, sat squatting that Fourth of July, 1919, in the 114-degree Toledo, Ohio, heat, bleeding, helpless, minus six teeth, his right cheek shattered and swollen to twice its normal size. "Jack the Giant Killer" had hammered in boxing's era of the knockout punch.

More attention swept over the new champion than had ever been visited upon an American boxer. In the country where prizefights were still illegal in many states, Dempsey was adored, fretted over, and editorialized about. Publications famous for their intellectuality or respectability found meaning in his intensity or goodness in his savage heart. Others brooded about the dark side of Dempsey's fighting nature and the American competitive spirit which responded to it.

The two greatest battles of Dempsey's heavyweight career, before Gene Tunney dealt out the final reckoning, made converts of his fascinated critics. Those who resented Dempsey's savage brilliance found their champion in Georges Carpentier of France, "The Orchid Kid," a war hero (Dempsey was accused of having been a draft-dodger) and a sleek high-liver with aristocratic tastes. Tex Rickard promoted the New Jersey fight—the first one-million-dollar gate in boxing history—as though civilization itself were at stake. The crowd was with the graceful Carpentier at first, but Dempsey's beautifully coordinated attack won

Dempsey takes on Georges Carpentier, 1921, Chicago Historical Society

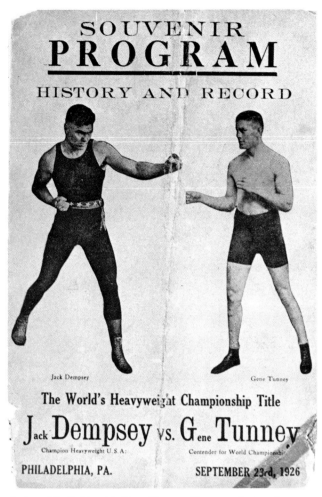

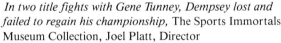

In two title fights with Gene Tunney, Dempsey lost and
failed to regain his championship, The Sports Immortals
Museum Collection, Joel Platt, Director

Together with Jack Dempsey, Tex Rickard
embodied the Golden Age of Boxing, Ring
Boxing Hall of Fame, New York

them over. Carpentier went down in the fourth, and Dempsey became the Golden Boy of the
Golden Age of boxing.

When he took on Luis Angel Firpo of Argentina, Dempsey faced the other side of
fighting. Firpo, "The Wild Bull of the Pampas," was a bruiser worthy of Dempsey's
pummeling style but without his "fighter's brain." When Argentina bull took on Colorado
mountain lion, the arena shook. After a savage first round, in which Dempsey floored Firpo
seven times and then was belted out of the ring, Dempsey came back, dazed and raging, and
knocked out Firpo in the second round. The 237-second bout, wrote one eyewitness, was
"the purest example of . . . sustained animosity in the history of glove fighting."

Dempsey's prowess brought him legendary purses, movie roles, and the adoration of men
and women. For three years after the Firpo match, he fought no one until Gene Tunney
laid down the challenge in 1926. Tunney's smooth, orchestrated style of defensive boxing
frustrated the aging champion's battering-ram attack and brought him, by decision, the
heavyweight crown. Dempsey came back for a rematch in 1927, which became known as the
"Battle of the Long Count," because his reluctance to return to his corner delayed the
referee's count and allowed Tunney to rise and later win the decision. The fans never forgot
Dempsey, who went on to become the most popular ex-champion in the history of boxing.
His savage fury forgotten, what lingered was the memory of a fighter who gave his all.
"That's what fans pay to see," he explained. "That's what makes fighting a good game. Take
it easy and you let everyone down."

TEX RICKARD (1871–1929)

Jack Dempsey once said that he was only 50 percent of the attraction for the hundreds of thousands of fans who paid top dollar to watch him take on all comers; the other 50 percent was one George Lewis "Tex" Rickard, promoter *extraordinaire,* whose brash, lavish, crowd-pleasing brand of hoopla made him, uniquely, a media star in a long line of backroom boys.

Dempsey laid them low; but Rickard made it matter. By the time two boxers came out swinging in a Rickard-promoted event during the 1920s, front pages were emptied of all other news, grandstands constructed overnight swayed ominously under the weight of record-breaking crowds (120,000 for the Dempsey–Carpentier classic), and millionaires, politicians, and movie stars scrambled for front-row seats. Not since the circuses of P. T. Barnum had America seen the like.

The country would have believed anything about the legendary Rickard, but his regiment of publicists didn't have to stray far from the truth. Born in a cabin in Missouri, the next farm over from Jesse James's mother's, Rickard made his way through a string of careers as Texas cowboy and town marshal, Yukon prospector, and owner of Klondike saloons—several of them lost on the turn of a card. The impresario of honky-tonk found his mission as a boxing promoter in Goldfield, Nevada. Anxious to put Goldfield on the map, he lured Battling Nelson, boxing's current glamour boy, to take on Joe Gans, "The Old Master." The purse was the largest in lightweight championship history and, to drive the point home, Rickard sent out photos of the $30,000 converted to stacks of newly minted twenty-dollar gold coins.

Always one to exploit a dramatic situation—or to manufacture one—Rickard later coaxed Jim Jeffries out of retirement to save the honor of the white race in the battle with black heavyweight champion Jack Johnson. The white race lost, but not Rickard. When, in 1919, he found in young Jack Dempsey a champion worthy of his flamboyance, there was no stopping him. To bring in the crowds, he manufactured a morality play in which the dark, scowling Dempsey was matched against the square-jawed champion of France, Georges Carpentier, and then a gladiatorial contest between Dempsey and Luis Firpo. Rickard's string of unprecedented one-million-dollar gates reached a triumphant peak when the re-match between a defeated Dempsey and a clean Gene Tunney wrung from an excited public $2,658,000.

Rickard found his ultimate monument in Madison Square Garden. The old Garden, a bankrupt white elephant, was revived after six months of Rickard's management. A six-day bicycle race brought out one hundred thousand spectators; big-league hockey was introduced to New York; and the Friday-night fight became an institution. When Rickard put up a new, grand Madison Square Garden, New York—and the United States—finally had its temple of sport. After his death in 1929, Rickard was laid out, in a fifteen-thousand-dollar bronze casket under the arena's arc lights, worshiped by the thousands who filed by as the master promoter of American romance.

◄ *Tex Rickard,* Ring Boxing Hall of Fame, New York

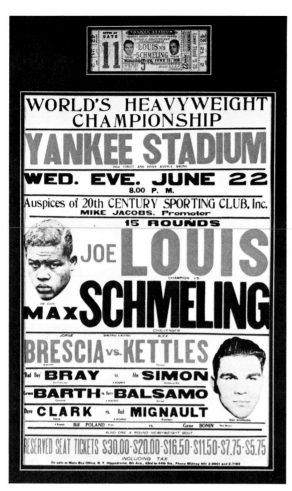

On June 22, 1938, Joe Louis—then
champion—had a rematch with his nemesis,
Max Schmeling, Daniel S. Turner

Joe Louis, Betsy Graves Reyneau,
Oil on canvas, 1946, National Portrait
Gallery, Smithsonian Institution

The Brown Bomber: *With sporting and political worlds paying rapt attention, Joe Louis avenged his defeat two years earlier at the hands of Max Schmeling,* Robert Riggs, Oil on canvas, c. 1940, Capricorn Galleries, Bethesda, Maryland

JOE LOUIS (1914–1981)

Has there ever been a knockout in boxing history more satisfying than Joe Louis's KO of the German Max Schmeling on June 22, 1938? Schmeling, a decent enough man in his own right, entered the ring as Hitler's champion of Aryan supremacy; Joe Louis, the first black heavyweight to win the support of the entire boxing public, took him on in the name of all the democratic values. A sweet 124 seconds after the battle of the surrogates began, Schmeling fell victim to Louis's cold fury, unleashing a night of rejoicing in both the black and white neighborhoods of America. "The Brown Bomber" had done it for them all.

The champ earned $349,288 that night, which one sportswriter calculated to be about $2,800 per second, but Louis had other reasons to savor the moment. His triumph erased a debt to his own pride. Two years before, almost to the day, Schmeling had laid the victor of twenty-seven consecutive fights senseless in the twelfth round. Louis never forgot or forgave the humiliation. "I won't be champion," he said after taking the heavyweight title from James Braddock the following year, "until I get that Schmelin'."

Schmeling's defeat, however, brought a new problem for Louis. In perfect fighting trim, the youngest boxer to win the heavyweight championship had trouble finding contenders worthy of his talents. Eager to fight, he took on everyone in what cynics called his "Bum of the Month Club." Impatient fans muttered that Louis was picking only second-raters to bring in money at little risk, but the truth was that Louis was too good—possibly the greatest champion ever. Blessed with superb fighter's instincts and an icy-calm temperament, he landed his punches at will. Finally, after three and a half years of bum-rushing, he was given a run for his money by Billy Conn. The 1941 fight brought Louis, dazzled by Conn's lightning footwork, within a hair of defeat. But power won out in the thirteenth-round knockout—just ahead of the bell.

After a stint in the Army, Louis polished off Conn in a return match but then faced a hint of his own mortality. On December 5, 1947, just over ten years after he had taken the championship, his reflexes gave way in a battle with "Jersey Joe" Walcott, which the judges in an unpopular decision nevertheless awarded Louis. He registered a clear victory against Walcott, six months later, in his twenty-fifth title defense and then, on March 1, 1949, called it quits.

The champion's reluctance to give up, which had sparked his brilliant comebacks after the Schmeling defeat and the Conn and Walcott scares, led to a serious miscalculation after his retirement. In debt to the government for back taxes, he returned to the ring, and to a defeat at the hands of Ezzard Charles. Louis swore he'd never fight again, but he didn't mean it until his decisive drubbing by his greatest successor, Rocky Marciano. Louis finally retired and let the memories of his ring brilliance take over. A great favorite among sportswriters, Louis earned their permanent respect as much for his honesty of character as for his fighting ability. "He acted," wrote Paul Gallico, "as though prize fighting were a sacred calling."

Rocky Marciano puts an end to Joe Louis's career in the ring, Ring Boxing Hall of Fame, New York

*Rocky Marciano in train-
ing before his 1955 bout
with Archie Moore,*
Hy Peskin, Photograph,
1955, Sports Illustrated

ROCKY MARCIANO (1924–1969)

Well before Rocky Marciano took the heavyweight championship in 1952, Hollywood had
already worked and reworked the film cliché of the tough young boxer with the heart of
gold. But only with Marciano did the boxing public get a champion who made it all seem
real. "The Brockton Blockbuster" was tough but not mean—a hard-hitter, with a
devastating right-hand punch he called his "Susie Q," who fought to win but not to
humiliate.

Marciano's power and his compassion first stirred the fans when he put an end to Joe
Louis's comeback hopes. The two fighters played out the classic struggle between young
scrapper and aging pro until Louis hit the canvas with such finality that the referee did not
bother to count him out. Marciano called it "the saddest punch of my life. How else could
I feel seeing . . . one of the finest sportsmen that ever lived lying there on the canvas?"
Louis believed him. "When he defeated me," he later said, "I think it hurt him more than it
hurt me."

But none of Marciano's opponents ever made the mistake of thinking that he was soft.

A mauler in the Sullivan–Dempsey tradition, he put one fighter, Carmine Vingo, into the hospital unconscious, and gave Jersey Joe Walcott the fight of his life on the championship night in Philadelphia, September 23, 1952. Marciano was so good that he was knocked down—but never out—only two times in his career. Walcott administered the first reminder that the Brockton, Massachusetts, fighter could be mortal early in the championship bout but, twelve rounds later, Marciano finally connected—as he always did—and Walcott went down. The new champion had never lost a professional fight up to that point—and he never would.

Of the five challengers Rocky took on during his reign of terror as champion, only Ezzard Charles was able to stay upright the full fifteen rounds. And even Charles dropped in a rematch three months later. Marciano might have gone on forever, but he decided to call it quits, undefeated, after he had proven himself equal to the elegant jabs of the finest scientific fighter of his day, Archie Moore, holder of the light heavyweight title.

Boxing commentators marveled at Marciano's willingness to retire in his prime, despite his potential to make millions more in the ring. But the fighter, who had already earned more than $1,400,000, left the limelight for the sake of his family, living out to the last his reputation as a boxer with perspective. Victor of all forty-nine of his professional fights, forty-five by knockout, he was shrewd enough never to attempt a comeback in the thirteen years left to him before he died in an airplane crash in 1969.

Ezzard Charles seen falling victim to Marciano's relentless attack,
Mark Kauffman, Photograph, 1954, Sports Illustrated

The Yacht America *Winning the Royal Yacht Club Cup at Cowes, 1851,* Fitzhugh Lane, after a sketch
by Oswald W. Brierly, Oil on canvas, 1851, The Peabody Museum, Salem, Massachusetts

YACHTING

Biographies by
AMY HENDERSON

JOHN C. STEVENS
First Commodore 1844-1854

John C. Stevens, Attributed to Charles Loring Elliott, Oil on canvas, c. 1860, New York Yacht Club

JOHN COX STEVENS (1785–1857)

A wealthy financier with a passion for yachting, John Cox Stevens was one of the most famous sports patrons of the mid-nineteenth century. He came from a family inextricably tied to the history of early American transportation. His father, Colonel John Stevens, pioneered steam travel in the United States, and his brothers—Edwin and Robert—were important inventors and shipbuilders. In the 1840s, when steam-powered ships were overtaking sailing packets and clipper ships as the carriers of American commerce, John Cox Stevens and his brothers began to develop yachting as a pleasure sport. Before 1840, yachts had simply been modeled after commercial and fishing vessels, but, as redesigned by the Stevenses, they were transformed into distinctive racing craft. Clubs were organized in such cities as Boston, Charleston, Detroit, and New Orleans, but the most important was formed in New York in 1844, with John Cox Stevens as its first commodore.

The most famous yacht race in history took place six years later. In 1851, England was planning to hold the world's first trade fair, a "Great Exhibition," intended by Prince Albert to show off the scientific and industrial progress of the age. Coincidentally, in February of that year, Lord Wilton, Commodore of the Royal Yacht Squadron, invited Commodore Stevens to visit the English Club at Cowes. The Americans leaped at the chance to trumpet their sailing prowess in the year of England's Great Exhibition, and a syndicate of New York Yacht Club members, headed by Stevens, was formed to commission the design and construction of a competition yacht. The *America* was delivered to the NYYC in June: a typical New York pilot boat, 101′9″ long over all, 90′3″ at the water line, with a 23-foot beam and an 11-foot draft. It carried 5,263 feet of sail on a revolutionary rig.

A professional crew sailed the *America* to France in the summer of 1851, where the sixty-six-year-old Stevens took command. They crossed the English Channel to Cowes, and were immediately met by a swift seventy-ton English cutter. The *Laverock* challenged the Yankee upstart to a race, and Stevens later explained that there had been no escape, "for the *Laverock* stuck to us." He said, "We were loaded with extra sails, with beef and port and bread enough for an East Indian voyage, and were some four or five inches too deep in the water." Yet the *America* managed to win this first English encounter by a quarter of a mile. Stevens and his crew then sat at anchor off Cowes for three weeks, waiting for someone to take up the challenge he had sent to Lord Wilton: ten thousand guineas to any ship that could beat the *America*. When no one took up the gauntlet, Stevens decided to enter the open race held by the Royal Yacht Squadron on August 22. Starting off the harbor at Cowes and racing around the Isle of Wight and back, his ship took an early lead, which she never relinquished, and handily won the "Hundred Guinea Cup." Legend has it that when a signalman on shore yelled out "Sail ho!" Queen Victoria—present to award the Cup—asked "Which boat is it?" "The *America,* Madam." "Oh, indeed. And which is second?" After a slight pause, the signalman answered, "I regret to report that there is no second." The London *Times* hailed the American victory as the "triumph of the year."

The America's Cup,
New York Yacht Club

Stevens returned the Hundred Guinea Cup to the United States and kept it in his Washington Square drawing room. When he died in the summer of 1857, the surviving members of the syndicate transferred the Cup—now rechristened the "America's Cup"—to the New York Yacht Club. It was to be a perpetual challenge cup, "for friendly competition between foreign countries," but it has never been lost by the United States.

BUS MOSBACHER (b. 1922)

In September 1962, crack skipper Emil "Bus" Mosbacher capped his sailing career by successfully defending the America's Cup—the closest thing in sports to the Holy Grail. What had begun in 1851 as a gentlemen's lark became in the twentieth century a proving-ground for sailing's technocrats. But it is still the contest itself which counts most. An affair of national pride, the race for the old Victorian ewer—the Hundred Guinea America's Cup—remains as great a public spectacle as ever. In the demands it puts on man and boat, it is the pinnacle.

The New York Yacht Club adopted the twelve-meter design for Cup races in the mid-1950s, a radical change from the larger "J"-class yachts which had dominated racing for decades. Post–World War II economics had dictated the scaling down, and the 1958 America's Cup contest was the first series to be run with the twelve-meters. The swifter boats were made to order for a gifted skipper like Mosbacher, who had cut his teeth in small-boat racing. Premiums in his class were placed on skill, daring, imagination—and money. In 1958, the cost of racing a twelve-meter during the summer Cup trials approached a million dollars. It was the sort of thing, one yachtsman rued, that "cuts into your drinking money."

Mosbacher, the best of this new breed of small-boat skippers, had been winning since he was a teenager in the 1930s. In one tight race when he was fifteen, the finish was so close that he yelled out a sportsmanlike "Nice race!" to his opponent, who yelled back, "Thank you." "Bus" (short for Buster) thought that he had lost, but one of his crew—a girl named Ethel—was furious. "Next thing I knew," he reported, "Ethel was standing up, shaking her fist at the committee boat and screaming, 'Ya blind bum, ya!' at the top of her lungs"—to considerable effect, since this girl was Ethel Merman. As it turned out, Bus had won.

In the 1950s, Mosbacher won the One-Design International class eight years in a row, a spectacular record which led to his selection as skipper of the twelve-meter *Vim* in the 1958 America's Cup trials. A much slower boat than its rival *Columbia,* which was eventually chosen to defend the Cup, *Vim* nevertheless put up a tremendous fight before losing out. In one tacking duel—and this was in the days before linked coffee-grinder winches made life aboard ship a lot easier—Mosbacher recalled, "Our boys were spitting up blood from exhaustion." He was very particular about his crews: "A good crew should serve as assistant eyes, but only to give me information. I give the only orders. It is not a democracy." But he was no Captain Bligh, and in fact was known for his cool restraint. "My crew knows something is wrong when they see tears coming down my cheeks."

It has been said of Mosbacher that he is the sort of fellow "who might make a milkshake instead of a martini . . . never smokes a cigarette, and always squeezes the toothpaste from the bottom." On land, he is the quintessential gentleman, with the kind of impeccable manners and gregarious good humor which, from 1969 to 1972, made him a highly popular United States chief of protocol. But on water he becomes transformed into a "blocky, blue-eyed bandit," as *Time* has described him, and his perpetual wide grin takes on a "saber-toothed quality." In match racing, he has said, "the idea is to find your opponent's Achilles' heel—and sink your teeth into it."

Mosbacher has defended the America's Cup twice. In 1962 he successfully skippered *Weatherly* against a faster Australian challenger, *Gretel,* and in 1967 he took *Intrepid* to victory in four straight races against the Australian *Dame Pattie.*

◀ *Bus Mosbacher at the helm,* Stanley Rosenfeld, Photograph, Collection of the photographer

A bicycle race, Calvert Lithograph Company, 1895, Library of Congress

BICYCLING

Biography by
AMY HENDERSON

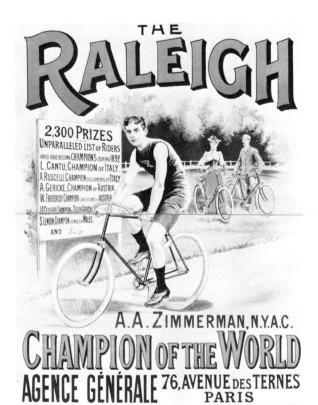

The world-renowned A. A. Zimmerman appeared on this 1892 Raleigh poster, Lorne Shields Cycling Collection, Ontario, Canada

Zimmerman and His Machine,
Henri de Toulouse-Lautrec,
Lithograph, 1895,
Boston Public Library

A. A. ZIMMERMAN (1869-1936)

It has been said that Americans rediscovered the wheel in the late nineteenth century. The invention of the "safety bicycle" in 1884—similar in design to today's bicycles and a radical departure from previous high-wheeled "boneshakers"—precipitated the cycling boom and provoked a virtual social revolution. Historians of the sport have said that "America went mad with the bicycle." Though originally popularized by gentleman amateurs, bicycling quickly grew into a general phenomenon. Mass production of the machines made cycling accessible to all levels of society—including women, who took it up as their first major outdoor sport. Philadelphia police became cyclists—to chase cycling robbers—and bicycles were adapted for use on railroad tracks and ice. Thousands of fresh-air enthusiasts belonged to touring clubs, but it was bicycle racing that especially captured America's fancy. Crowds of up to thirty thousand packed racetracks from Worcester, Massachusetts, to Ottumwa, Iowa, and riders tried to outperform one another in thrilling and reckless feats of derring-do. By the 1890s, bicycle racing had become the most popular spectator sport in the country.

A. A. Zimmerman was the idol of the racing world. Born in Camden, New Jersey, he began cycle racing in 1889 and became an international star within three years. In 1893 "Zimmy" (as he liked to be called) won the first World Sprint Championship, initiating his decade-long and worldwide domination of the sport. Though his bicycle was heavier and less sleek than today's machines, and his tires far inferior, he established records that have respectability even by contemporary standards. Zimmerman trained hard during the racing season, cycling ten miles at high speed in morning, afternoon, and evening intervals—this at a time when most track riders raced only on Sundays, the day of their matches. His off-season (October to March) weight often climbed to more than 180 pounds but, in condition, the six-foot Zimmerman was a lean 160 pounds or less. His long and heavily muscled legs were perfect for cycle sprinting, and in his prime he was absolute master of the sport. During one match in France, he won so easily that the officials asked him to try something different in the next race to make things more interesting. "After the bell," he responded. In a field with three French cyclists, Zimmerman was dead last for three of the four laps of the race. When the bell was sounded to announce the fourth lap, he still held back—until the final turn. Then, in an astonishing burst of energy and skill, he exploded past the other riders to win the race by twenty meters.

In 1893, while still an amateur, Zimmerman won fifteen bicycles, fifteen diamonds, fourteen medals, two cups, seven pairs of studs, eight watches, one city lot, six clocks, four scarfpins, nine pieces of silverware, two bronzes, two wagons, one piano, and more. The next year, he turned professional, and won more than a hundred races in France, England, Ireland, and Germany. Lionized wherever he went, he was once asked, by the governor-general's wife in Australia, to demonstrate the art of bicycle riding in the ballroom of the palace. He also proved to be a shrewd businessman, and lent his name to "Zimmy" shoes, "Zimmy" toe clips, and "Zimmy" clothing.

A newspaper reported in 1896 that "Mr. A. A. Zimmerman stands alone as the greatest racer the world has produced . . . the champion of the world in competitive contests where brain, brawn, and muscle necessarily combine for supremacy."

The Kentucky Derby, 1977, Neil Leifer, Photograph, Sports Illustrated

HORSE RACING

Biographies by
MARC PACHTER

Hiram Woodruff,
Unidentified artist,
Oil on canvas,
Date unknown,
Hall of Fame of
the Trotter, Goshen,
New York

HIRAM WOODRUFF (1817–1867)

In the middle of the nineteenth century—before baseball, prizefighting, amateur athletics, and big-time thoroughbred racing would rise to dominate the field—trotting was the great American sport, and Hiram Woodruff its greatest figure. The trotter's diagonal gait (right front and left rear legs moving together, followed by left front and right rear legs), which had been developed by breeders to allow the pulling of wagons without swaying, was rooted in rural and small-town America. Patriotic Americans, opposed to the aristocratic, European tradition of racing thoroughbreds at a gallop, could still satisfy their fascination with speed in the homely tradition of trotting meets at agricultural fairs, and at a new series of tracks opened in mid-century. "Horse racing," pronounced Oliver Wendell Holmes, Sr., "is not a republican institution; horse trotting is."

Woodruff was the Renaissance man of American trotting. Breeder of the finest stock in the world, he was also celebrated as a master of all styles of racing at a trot: "under saddle," "in harness" (the pulling of a two-wheel sulky), and "to wagon" (the pulling of a four-wheel vehicle). Trained to the sport by his uncle, director of the country's first great course at Philadelphia, and by his father, superintendent of the Harlem track, in New York City, the future "Napoleon of the Trotting Turf" made his reputation, as a twenty-one-year-old, with Dutchman, an ugly animal of extraordinary speed. Woodruff's challenge, "Dutchman against the World," led to a match with a leading rival and a record-breaking run of 7 minutes 41 seconds, ahead of the standing three-mile time in harness by 26 seconds. Woodruff's showmanship provoked another record. A crowd, numbered in the thousands, turned out in the summer of 1839 at Beacon Course in Hoboken, New Jersey, to watch Dutchman, Woodruff up, racing alone "against Time" to establish a three-circuit record of 7 minutes $32\frac{1}{2}$ seconds—unbeaten for the next thirty-three years. Perhaps to prove the expertise of his racing technique, Hiram sold Dutchman the following year. Immediately thereafter, the trotter began to lose.

So powerful was the impression that Woodruff made on the racing public that his appearance in a race could seriously upset the betting odds. "It's twenty to thirty percent in favor of any horse that Hiram Woodruff rides," reported a contemporary. In an era when few drivers were likely to pass up offers to fix a race, it was said of him that "he could not even think a rascality, and rascals as well as honest men knew it." Although America had not yet developed the habit of sports-hero worship, the noble Woodruff inspired some genteel early attempts: "When he walked through his stables," wrote one admirer, "the undoubted accord which he had established with its glossy inmates was at once evinced by low whinnies of welcome which would greet his kindly presence as he went from stall to stall."

By the time Woodruff had settled into his glory as "The Old Field Marshal," veteran of more than thirty years in trotting, he had one more marvel to unleash on the world: his last, and greatest, horse, Dexter. "Here," the trainer said with characteristic showmanship, "is the horse that will make the best trotter we have ever seen—the King of the World." Although Woodruff died in 1867, before Dexter's career was over, he had the satisfaction of seeing the first three years of Dexter's record string of forty-nine victories out of fifty-three contests. It was a remarkable finish.

Grey Eagle Driven by Hiram Woodruff, Esq., N. Currier, Lithograph, 1850, Library of Congress

ISAAC MURPHY (1859?–1896)

Color was no bar for Isaac Murphy when he decided upon a career as a jockey. But age unquestionably was. About two years shy of qualifying legitimately for training (his exact birthdate is unknown), he pretended to be sixteen years old in 1875—the inaugural year of the Kentucky Derby—and won his first race within months. It was a natural enough choice of career. Murphy had been born in the heart of horse country, in Fayette County, Kentucky, where blacks dominated the jockey ranks, and he weighed in at about 90 pounds. But he was a natural in still another sense, demonstrating early a rapport with his mounts which came to be legendary. Because of it, the young jockey would one day retire a wealthy man, victor of 628 out of 1,412 races. His winning average of 44 percent has never been equaled.

Regularly described as "imperturbable" in the sporting press, Murphy became famous on the racetracks of the South, Midwest, and East for his low-key style as a rider. Surrounded by anxious jockeys bent low over their mounts, whipping and spurring them into a frenzy, he was easily recognizable sitting upright in the saddle coaxing, but not driving, his horse on. Murphy sensed the full extent of his mount's stamina and the point he might call upon it for the final push. Master of the grandstand finish, he brought enormous excitement to nineteenth-century racetracks. "No man with a touch of heart disease," cautioned one writer, "should ever back his mounts."

As a track phenomenon, Murphy had no equals among his contemporaries. His greatest competition for honors in the history of the sport would come from jockeys not yet born during his heyday. Murphy won the American Derby in Chicago four times in five years, including the first three run. In the twentieth century, Eddie Arcaro would win an equal number, but over a longer period. Murphy won the preeminent Kentucky Derby three times—in 1884 riding Buchanan, in 1890 riding Riley, and in 1891 riding Kingman. That record would endure for nearly forty years until 1930, when it was tied by Earl Sande, and would not be broken for sixty years, when it was surpassed by Arcaro. Murphy's record of five wins at Kentucky's Latonia Derby still stands. "He's the great one," admitted his finest rival, jockey Ed "Snapper" Garrison. "I've got to admit it."

Garrison's uncharacteristic humility was shaped during one of the great races of the late nineteenth century: a challenge match between the four-year-olds Tenny, Garrison up, and Salvator, Murphy up, at Sheepshead Bay, New York, on June 25, 1890. Tenny's owner, D. T. Pulsifer, dissatisfied with a defeat the week before, had asked Salvator's owner, James Ben Ali Haggin, to match a purse of $5,000 for another go. Thrilled by the sporting proposition, a full crowd turned out to watch two great jockeys of clashing styles—Murphy, as a reporter for the *Spirit of the Times* described him, "sitting steady as a rock, so immovable he might have been a figure of wood," and Garrison, a man of "cyclonic fury," roused to "desperate efforts." Murphy's calm and judgment won the day, leading one excited spectator to deliver herself of a widely reprinted poem: "We are under the string now—the great race is done/And Salvator, Salvator, Salvator won!"

Murphy, a national celebrity, retired a few years later, at the end of the era of black dominance in his sport. In 1896, the year of Murphy's untimely death of pneumonia, a black jockey, William L. Simms, became the first American to win an English race. But by 1902 the Kentucky Derby had seen its last black victor, Jim Winkfield. "They came and they dominated," Winkfield said years later. And then they were gone.

Jockey Isaac Murphy,
J. H. Fenton, Photograph,
1885, Library of Congress

Below:
Great Horses in a Great Race:
*Murphy on Salvator in the great
match race of the 1890s,*
Currier & Ives, Lithograph, 1891,
Library of Congress

AUGUST BELMONT II (1853–1924)

Autocrat of the racing stable, August Belmont II put the stamp of his personality on a sport struggling to achieve order in the late nineteenth and early twentieth centuries. By the time of his ascendancy as owner and breeder of thoroughbreds in the 1890s, the first attempts to standardize the rules of racing and to set the priorities of the racing calendar were launched by institutions dominated by his leadership. As a member of the first New York State Racing Commission, and as chairman of the all-powerful New York Jockey Club from 1895 (one year after its founding) until his death in 1924, Belmont controlled the licensing of jockeys and trainers, the appointment of racetrack officials, the allotment of racing dates, and the protection of thoroughbred bloodlines.

Belmont's own stables were the bedrock of his authority. Uninterested in thoroughbreds until after the death of his illustrious father, the nation's leading horse breeder, in 1890, he set about restocking the family's Nursery Stud on Long Island. There, and later at his farm near Lexington, Kentucky, he bred a string of champions—eight of them winners of $100,000 or more, a record for the day. The glory of his stable was Man O' War, sired by Fair Play and sold as a yearling, who would be celebrated as the greatest thoroughbred America has ever produced.

Belmont and Horse, Unidentified artist, Bronze, Date unknown, The National Museum of Racing, Inc., Saratoga Springs, New York

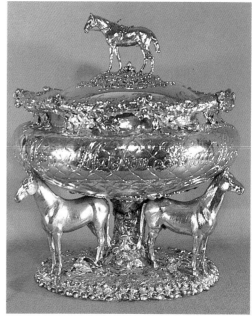

The Belmont Cup,
New York Racing Association

Left:
August Belmont II, Théobald Chartran,
Oil on canvas, 1893, The National
Museum of Racing, Inc., Saratoga
Springs, New York

In 1902, Belmont guided the Westchester Racing Association in its purchase of a large tract of 650 acres in Queens, Long Island. Three years later, the association opened the country's most majestic racecourse and named it after August Belmont, Sr. The track's grandeur was as much a monument to the opulent taste of its president as it was to the memory of his father. Graced by a luxurious clubhouse, with elaborate dining rooms, bedrooms, and balconies, Belmont Park offered a 650-foot grandstand, a track a mile and a half in circumference, and an adjacent training area. Successful at first, the Park would later survive years of anti-betting laws, imposed by the New York legislature, only through the ingenuity of its president.

No one ever called August Belmont a man of the people. Kingpin of an aristocratic sport in an aristocratic age, he carried the prerogatives of his class and his position within the racing community with cold, persuasive dignity. But there was flair in the scope of his initiatives and in the confidence of his leadership. In the history of thoroughbred racing, he was the last of his kind. "Men equally prominent, equally powerful . . . within their own orbits, and men more successful in racing financially were to come along later," concluded racing historian William Robertson, "but the day of nationwide domination by individuals ended with Belmont."

A mud-bespattered Earl Sande,
National Portrait Gallery,
Smithsonian Institution

Batteau, Earl Sande Up, Richard
B. Adams, Oil on canvas, 1903,
Mr. and Mrs. Walter M. Jeffords

EARL SANDE (1898–1968)

Earl Sande was a jockey tailor-made for the hoopla of the 1920s. He had the reputation of a winner—and the era loved a winner above all things. Of his more than 3,600 starts in an on-again-off-again career which began during the First World War and effectively ended by the mid-1930s, Sande placed in the money 60 percent, and in the winner's circle 27 percent, of the time. One memorable day—at Havre de Grace in Maryland—he rode six straight winners to victory. In his pinnacle year of 1923, Sande triumphed in thirty-nine stakes races. It would take three decades, when there were four times as many races in a season, for another jockey to catch up. His total purse that year was $569,394 (out of a lifetime estimate of $3,000,000)—of which Sande took 10 percent. The Earl of Sande had the air of someone doing well, and the crowds warmed to his cockiness.

Sande's three victories at the Kentucky Derby—tying the great Isaac Murphy—were the sweetest of his career. The first, in 1923, came in the face of miserable odds. His horse, Zev, had placed a contemptible twelfth in the Preakness and—the rumors went—had been sneaked into the Derby lineup only at Sande's urgent request. With the odds an insulting 19 to 1 against him, Zev took an early lead and stayed in front to win by one and a half lengths. Sportswriter and sometime poet Damon Runyon gave the national cheer:

> Green an' white at the home-stretch—
> Who do you think'll win?
> Who but a handy
> Guy like Sande
> Kickin' that baby in!

The next victory, in 1925, was the most satisfying of all. One year before, Sande had suffered a serious accident at Saratoga. His ribs and collarbone broken, his left leg crushed, he had spent several months in the hospital reading obituaries for his career. Some concluded that even should he recover physically, he could never be expected to recover his nerve. But at the next Derby, Sande was up again, riding Flying Ebony. Neither horse nor jockey was highly rated. His victory, the comeback of the decade, was toasted throughout the country as every American's dream of beating overwhelming odds.

Sande's retirement three years later set the stage for his final Kentucky Derby triumph. After an unsuccessful try at life as a trainer, and a crushing loss in the stock market crash, the great jockey returned to the headlines riding the Derby favorite, Gallant Fox. This time he rode *with* the odds to an easy two-length victory and earned another few lines from Runyon:

> Say, have they turned the pages
> Back to the past once more,
> Back to the racin' ages?
> An' Derby out of the yore?
> Say, don't tell me I'm daffy!
> Ain't that the same ol' grin?
> Why, it's that handy
> Guy named Sande
> Bootin' a winner in.

When Sande retired, a few years later, to try his luck again as a trainer, he made it stick—for at least a few decades. In 1953 he was news again, a fifty-four-year-old jockey, making a last comeback at Belmont, scene of five of his victories. The glory days were clearly over, but Sande made a respectable third-place showing. "I got a little tired," he said philosophically, "and so did the horse."

Woodward stable colors worn by Sande, The National Museum of Racing, Inc., Saratoga Springs, New York

116

JAMES FITZSIMMONS (1874–1966)

Devotees of the racetrack like to tell about the time when James Fitzsimmons—"Mr. Fitz"
to those who worked with him in the training stables—was approached by the legendary
boxing manager of the 1920s, Doc Kearns, and his new find, Jack Dempsey. Mr. Fitz
stepped back from the fighter, looked him over from head to toe, and announced, as Jimmy
Breslin reports it: "Look at him. Built for speed. Oh, you can see that. Don't have to know
much to see that you're built for speed, boy." As Fitzsimmons saw it, there was no difference
between athletes and thoroughbreds. "I suppose there are many ways to measure greatness,"
he once wrote. "In humans the yardstick may be individual courage. . . . Horsemen measure
thoroughbreds by the same quality." That respect was the mark of his stables. Anyone who
saw one of Mr. Fitz's prime horses—above all Nashua, the pride of his old age—return from
a morning workout surrounded by an army of grooms brushing away flies and rubbing in
liniment, understood how deeply the old man admired his champions.

Fitzsimmons might well have become a track legend just by growing old in the
profession. At the time of his retirement in 1963, before his eighty-ninth birthday, "The Grand
Old Man of American Racing" had spent more than three-quarters of a century in the sport.
But, long before his canonization as sage and symbol of a rich tradition, the young
Fitzsimmons was already a darling of the racing press. His disposition had something to do
with it. "Sunny Jim they ought to call him," suggested a New York reporter, christening him
in the press forever. He was also a celebrated racetrack "character," easy to spot in his

suspenders, his baggy pants, his old hat. But, though Sunny Jim was "not particular about the color effect when it came to neckties," as one wag put it, he was recognized as the best public trainer in the country, and owners who might have hired a full-time trainer of their own boarded their horses with him and gave up 10 percent of all stakes and purses won for the privilege. The press had first begun to notice Fitzsimmons in 1914 when James Johnson, owner of the Quincy Stable, handed over his thirty-four horses. Ten years later, Sunny Jim was put in charge of the illustrious William Woodward stable, Belair Stud, and of the Wheatley Stable owned by Mrs. Henry Phipps and her brother, Ogden Mills. Between the two stables, "he was to have," wrote Breslin, "as close to a corner on the racing market as you could get."

During the heyday of the Woodward–Fitzsimmons association, jockeys carried the silks of Belair Stud, white with red spots, to victory in most of the classics. Half of the winners in a ten-year period at the Belmont Stakes—a record number—had been bred by Woodward and trained by Fitzsimmons. Mr. Fitz's champions also took the honors at the Kentucky Derby in 1930, 1935, and 1939. Two of them, Gallant Fox in 1930 and Omaha in 1935, won the Triple Crown, garnering victories in the Preakness and the Belmont Stakes as well. Fitzsimmons never saw one of his Derby winners come in. All three times his view was blocked by the excited crowds.

Still going strong in the 1950s, Mr. Fitz had the satisfaction of seeing Nashua win the Preakness and the Belmont Stakes in 1955, and then outrun the Derby winner, Swaps, in a ballyhooed "match of the century"—$100,000 winner-take-all. It was an amazing achievement for horse and trainer alike. The year before, two-year-old Nashua had shown his potential in the Futurity and reminded the world that the old man was still a force to be reckoned with. "Look at him," someone said, pointing to Sunny Jim walking by. "In what other business could an eighty-year-old man win something called the Futurity?"

Nashua: *This great horse, his trainer, "Sunny Jim," and jockey Eddie Arcaro formed the wonder team of American thoroughbred racing in 1955,* W. Smithson Broadhead, Oil on canvas, 1955, The National Museum of Racing, Inc., Saratoga Springs, New York

EDDIE ARCARO (b. 1916)

No one can define exactly what it is that makes a jockey great. "It's like playing a piano," explained Ben Jones, trainer of 1948's wonder horse, Citation. "Some have a better touch than others." He was thinking of Eddie Arcaro, twice winner of racing's Triple Crown, who had just brought Citation in for the roses at the Kentucky Derby. Arcaro would put in another thirteen years on the track, but he was already "The Master" to his fellow jockeys, and a legend to the spectators who would count on him to bring the thoroughbreds home. Eddie never worried about how much horse and how much driver went into the winning combination. The trick was to make them inseparable: "You've got to make the horse think that you're part of him. You sit right tight and dig your hands into his neck. And when he drives, you drive, and when he comes back, you come back with him."

The trick did not come easily. Part of the Arcaro legend is the story, much embellished, of his slow start. One authority had it that Arcaro raced 250 times before riding a winner; others stuck to the more conservative estimate of 100. The talk finally got to Arcaro, who had the record books checked: forty-five mounts, it was, before his first win on January 14, 1932. No matter. Once he was launched, he would ride to a career total, over thirty-one years, of nearly five thousand winners, and many thousands more in the money. He credits horse owner Clarence Davison—who gave him three years of rigorous training—with making a competitor out of him.

His will to win sharpened, the young Arcaro became one of the most fearless athletes in a dangerous sport. "I figured that when I signed my name to be a jockey," he later wrote, "death might be a part of it. Every jockey should know that or get out." The word on the tracks during his first years of competitive racing was that the young jockey was "a kid who either had to be awfully lucky or get killed." It nearly happened at Chicago's Washington Park, on June 6, 1933, when Eddie's mount, Gun Fire, buckled and fell, throwing him under the hooves of a galloping horse. Unconscious for three days, Arcaro spent the next three months in a hospital nursing a fractured skull and punctured lung. It was the first of a lifetime string of near-misses. By his own estimate, Arcaro was thrown about fifty times.

The passion which kept him going also nearly ended his right to continue racing. Hot-tempered, ambitious, and rough-edged, he pulled a six-month suspension at Pimlico in 1936 for deliberately colliding with nearby horses, a charge he disputed, and then in 1941 was suspended again for blocking. The next charge was the one that almost finished his career. After his first Triple Crown year riding Whirlaway, Arcaro was locked, the autumn of 1942, in a furious race with jockey Vincenzo Nodarse at Aqueduct. Convinced that Nodarse had deliberately pushed him off stride, Arcaro went out after the Cuban rider, crowding him against the rail. "I tried to put him over the fence," he recalled years later, "and it was the luckiest thing that he didn't get killed." Still angry and unrepentant when confronted by racing authorities, he was handed an unlimited suspension.

One year later, he was back. The mature Arcaro kept the fire but not the fury. After a ten-year association with Mrs. Payne Whitney's Greentree Stable, he became a freelance in 1946 and celebrated with a Triple Crown two years later and with his fifth Derby win in 1952. The Arcaro passion continued to astonish the press. "With whip raised as the gate sprung," went one eyewitness account of the legendary 1955 Nashua–Swaps match race, "he lit into Nashua with the violence of a pneumatic drill. His open-mouthed battle cry [was] screamed out into the ears of the gate crew with the violence of a *banzai*." Six years later, "Heady Eddie" retired on his laurels. *Sports Illustrated* called him "the most famous man to ride a horse in America since Paul Revere."

Arcaro thrown by Black Hills during the Belmont Stakes, Herb Scharfman, Photograph, 1959, Sports Illustrated

Left:
Weighing In: *First version of what would become the* Saturday Evening Post *cover for June 28, 1958,* Norman Rockwell, Oil on canvas, 1958, Mr. and Mrs. Robert J. Chambers

◄ *Eddie Arcaro and Sunny Jim before a race at Hialeah,* John Walther, Photograph, 1957, Miami Herald

Willie Shoemaker,
Sheedy & Long, Photograph,
Sports Illustrated

WILLIE SHOEMAKER (b. 1931)

In horse racing, even more than in football (*pace* Vince Lombardi), winning is not everything; it is the only thing. Greatness in a jockey is measured year after year by the numbers—the horses he brings home to victory, the purses he collects. By that standard there has never been, and may never again be, a jockey like Willie Shoemaker. Off and running his first full year in the saddle, as an eighteen-year-old, he rode 219 winners, second-highest that year, and tied for first with 388 the next. By 1953 he had the look of a phenomenon. In October he passed the record for wins by a jockey in a single year, at 392, and went on to a total of 485. He might have gone on even further to 500, but he quit that season, with magnificent aplomb, to take a vacation.

Then he went out for the all-time records. In 1958 one writer speculated that the nine-year veteran was "the only jockey in the country who has even a remote chance of approaching Johnny Longden's record of 5,090 winners in 31 seasons." Longden retired nine years later with a final 6,032, and "The Shoe" was right behind him. In September 1970, he pulled ahead, topping the senior jockey in nearly half of Longden's forty seasons and with about 7,000 fewer than his 32,000 rides. Four years later, Willie was over the 7,000-victory mark and still riding. In 1972, one more jockey, his great friend Eddie Arcaro, was moved aside in the record books when Shoemaker, riding a winner at Santa Anita in his home state of California, passed Arcaro's notch of 554 stakes victories.

Shoemaker on Spectacular Bid,
Richard Stone Reeves, Oil
on canvas, 1980, Roy Gene
Evans and William M. Stuart

Throughout the growing excitement, Shoemaker has remained cool enough to be labeled by one admirer "The Iceman." Unemotional, unfailingly polite, and even deferential during much of his career, "Silent Shoe" has been the calm center of the stormy racing world. As a rider, his keynote is smoothness. "He's the master of the whole situation," observed a racing official, "and yet he never seems to be doing anything up there. He doesn't scrub and rub around on the horse. . . . He's like a little computer . . . knowing exactly when to do what and moving the horse with little clucks and touches." It has been said of the Shoe that all riders talk to their horses but that he is the only one horses talk back to.

As befits a great jockey, the race he rode that everyone remembers is the incredible one when Shoemaker made the only serious mistake of his career. On May 4, 1957—Derby Day—the Shoe, riding Gallant Man, stood up in the stirrups short of the finish line, permitting Iron Liege to win by a nose. "You can ask 100 people and 90 of them can tell you who lost that Derby," he later said, "but they can't tell you who won." Mistaking the sixteenth pole for the finish line was a monumental error, taking its place among the legends of the sport. But Shoemaker survived and flourished. "He's the only one I know who could have suffered that kind of experience in a race like the Derby without going to pieces," said Eddie Arcaro. "That's why the little son of a gun is going to go on and on."

During the 1960 Indy 500, eleven cars crashed and fourteen spectators were injured,
James R. Root, Photograph, Sports Illustrated

AUTO RACING

Biographies by
JEANNETTE HUSSEY

Barney Oldfield, most colorful of the early auto racing greats, Bettmann Archive, Inc.

BARNEY OLDFIELD (1878–1946)

Eighty-five years ago, at the outset of the American automobile adventure, the challenge was out to demonstrate that—for both endurance and speed—the car was better than the horse. Barney Oldfield proved the point and in the process became identified with speed and daredevil driving in America.

Oldfield was first a bicycle racer who once billed himself throughout the Midwest as "The Bicycle Champion of Ohio." His seventeen-year automobile racing career began at the Manufacturer's Challenge Cup race at Grosse Pointe, Michigan, on October 25, 1902. Perched behind the wheel of the famous "999," a car built by Tom Cooper and Henry Ford and named after the New York locomotive, Oldfield won the five-mile distance in 5 minutes 28 seconds. With a "roar like unto a passing comet," said *The Automobile* magazine, Oldfield "skidded around the far turn and flashed past the howling, horn-tooting crowd . . . in an exhibition that caused the whole great crowd to gulp and gasp." He later recalled the event as his greatest thrill. That race launched Barney Oldfield's career and also won for Henry Ford the financial backing to start his motorcar company. As for the spectators—they had witnessed the birth of a legend.

Oldfield earned his reputation chiefly as a showman. Barnstorming across the country, he cheered the hearts of county fair crowds with his dangerous, daredevil act and his boisterous shout, as he circled the track, "You know me, I'm Barney Oldfield!" In the "Green Dragon," a car built by the Peerless Company, Oldfield became known in 1904 as "The World's Champion Automobilist." Danger was his trade. Outfitted in a green leather suit and the ever-present unlit cigar in his mouth (a shock absorber to check the vibrations between his teeth), he appeared on tracks from coast to coast, beating all other racers. Said Oldfield that year: "There's just one thing which tempts me to go on risking my neck time and again. I'm a firm believer in the product and I always spell it with a capital M—for Money."

Outraged, the newly formed American Automobile Association suspended him for "outlaw" racing. But such restrictions failed to lessen Oldfield's public appeal. Occasionally he starred in a skit called *Vanderbilt Cup*, in which he played a poor mechanic who saved the day. In 1910 the AAA again suspended him for participating in a match race against Jack Johnson, then the world's heavyweight boxing champion. Despite the scorn of that organization, Oldfield—more than any other man—had popularized the automobile in the United States.

On the occasion of the first Indianapolis Speedway races, held in 1909, Oldfield was honored for the record he had set six years earlier as America's first mile-a-minute man. The following year, at Daytona Beach, he won international acclaim by setting one of the earliest world speed records in a big, chain-driven Blitzen Benz—he drove 131.724 mph. Later Oldfield described the experience: "I let the great machine have its head, and for fully a third of the distance the wheels were off the ground while I fought for control. The front wheels were shooting up and down in a weird dance, and I knew that if a tire burst I would be beyond mortal help. I shot through space until . . . I approached the verge of unconsciousness. Then I shut her down, knowing I had traveled faster than any other human on earth."

Oldfield driving a Maxwell at Venice, California, in 1915, The National Museum of American History, Smithsonian Institution

Ralph DePalma with his nephew Peter DePaolo, The National Museum
of American History, Smithsonian Institution

The Vanderbilt Cup trophy, which DePalma won in 1912 and 1914, The National Museum of American History, Smithsonian Institution

RALPH DePALMA (1883–1956)

America's first authentic driving champion began his initial race in reverse. Seated behind the wheel of an Allan-Kingston motorcar, on Memorial Day, 1907, Ralph DePalma backed his front wheels off the starting line just as the flag dropped. The following year, however, he established his name among pioneer drivers by defeating the great Barney Oldfield in several dirt track races at Readville, Massachusetts, beginning an intense rivalry.

The DePalma family had settled in Brooklyn after emigrating from Italy in 1893. Young Ralph was "bitten with the speed bug" at an early age and, like Oldfield, he began his career as a bicycle racer. But, while Oldfield's name became legend due to his showmanship, DePalma won fame for his sportsmanship. His cool balance of dignity and derring-do made him one of the most highly respected men in auto racing. President Theodore Roosevelt called him "the truest, cleanest sportsman I have ever had the pleasure of meeting."

DePalma's most spectacular race took place at the second Indianapolis Motor Speedway event in 1912 before a crowd of eighty thousand spectators. Driving a Mercedes, he was within a mile of winning the race when his already badly damaged engine failed completely. Courageous and determined, DePalma and his co-driver gamely pushed the big car, the famous "Grey Ghost," toward the finish line as Joe Dawson, the nearest competitor, roared past them to win the race and the twenty-thousand-dollar prize. DePalma won a tumultuous ovation from the stand, and the lingering image of his fighting spirit brought him fame. Three years later, he won the five-hundred-mile Indianapolis classic. In time, he would hold a long-standing record for leading in the most laps in Indianapolis Speedway history.

DePalma's triumph over Barney Oldfield, in the Vanderbilt Cup race in Santa Monica, California, in February 1914, was perhaps the most satisfying victory of his twenty-seven-year career. As Oldfield's Mercer was the faster of the two cars, DePalma relied on his wits rather than the old Grey Ghost Mercedes to win. Signaling a pit stop, he roared ahead instead, at top speed, while Oldfield—feeling safely in the lead—pitted, and was then unable to retrieve the lost time. The Oldfield–DePalma rivalry continued to attract crowds and to produce national and international records.

Between 1912 and 1930 Ralph DePalma was never out of the top ratings among the great racers. After World War I, at Daytona Beach, he set a new land speed record (faster than the flight records of the day) driving a V-12 Packard at 149.887 mph. Still racing at the age of forty-seven, he won the Canadian Championship in 1929. DePalma was the winner of twenty-nine national championship races—a record which remained unbroken until the 1960s.

WILBUR SHAW (1902–1954)

Wilbur Shaw's devotion to the sport of auto racing extended beyond participation in its great events. He launched a successful one-man crusade, after World War II, to preserve and renovate the neglected site of one of the world's greatest sports spectacles, the Indianapolis 500. A three-time winner of the Indy classic, Shaw won his first victory in a car he had built himself in 1937. Driving a 3-liter 8 CTF Maserati in 1939 and 1940, he became the first to win in two consecutive years. In 1941 Shaw again held the lead for five laps, but then a wheel hub broke and sent him crashing into the retaining wall. As president and general manager of the Indianapolis Speedway, from 1945 until 1954, he devoted the last nine years of his life to rejuvenating the most famous American track.

Victory at Indianapolis had always been Wilbur Shaw's prime objective. He first entered the classic in May 1927. "This was the big show," he wrote of the 500. "To me it was a world's series, a heavyweight championship fight, a National Open, Rose Bowl game and a Kentucky Derby all rolled into one tremendous spectacle—with a touch of the pomp and

Wilbur Shaw after his third Indianapolis victory, in 1940, Wide World Photos, Inc.

Shaw broke a record to win the 1937 Indy 500 in 4 hours, 24 minutes, 7.81 seconds.
His mechanic, Jigger Johnson (left), *sits with Shaw,* United Press International

ceremony of a coronation." Although his car lasted only forty-two laps, he was undaunted. Three times during the 1930s, he finished second. Early in the 1931 race, he crashed over the retaining wall in a Dusenberg. Uninjured, he returned to the pits and resumed the race as a relief driver for Jimmy Gleason. When his car again headed for the wall, missing it by a fraction of an inch, his mechanic turned white.

A school dropout, Shaw had been employed by the Stutz Company in Indianapolis. There he had educated himself in automobile engineering enough to build his own racing car, the "Imperial Special." But when he attempted to enter his first race, he was promptly told to get his "bag of bolts" off the track. Undiscouraged, he raced—and crashed—the car in another event, escaping injury by scooting down "into the basement" (under the cowl) and clinging to the steering column. The steering wheel of Shaw's next car—"Old Red"—had to be installed after he seated himself inside. For his racing debut, Shaw's friends sent him an ambulance filled with flowers. But in that glove-tight vehicle he stacked up many victories. "When my time finally comes," Shaw once told his friends, "it isn't going to matter whether I'm driving a race car, flying a plane, or sitting at home in an easy chair." He died in a plane crash in 1954.

The Indianapolis 500 trophy, Borg-
Warner Corporation/Indianapolis Motor
Speedway Hall of Fame Museum

*A. J. Foyt, after his fourth victory
at the Indy 500,* Heinz Kleutmeier,
Photograph, 1977, Sports Illustrated

A. J. FOYT (b. 1935)

"The total race driver, that's Foyt," said one associate about the man who was voted driver of the decade in the 1960s. "Never has there been a driver with such absolute urge to excel, the absolute need to win, fairly and honestly . . . skill against skill, flat out and belly to the ground." One of the most versatile of professional drivers, Foyt drives stock cars and sports cars as well as the big, open-cockpit cars. Seven times a national driving champion, beginning in 1960, he is a four-time winner of the Indy classic and the winner, in 1972, of the Daytona 500, the nation's top stock-car race. Foyt was also a member (with Dan Guerney) of the first United States team to win, in 1967, France's sports-car classic, the Twenty-Four Hours of Le Mans.

The son of a midget-car racer, A. J. Foyt possesses a natural talent, great confidence, and an inordinate desire to win automobile races. He began racing at the age of eleven. After conquering the tracks of his native Texas, he entered national competition. In 1958 young Foyt qualified, and placed sixteenth in the Indianapolis five-hundred-mile race.

The element of unpredictability makes the Indy 500 one of the most exciting of all sporting events. Drivers who were certain to win have experienced—during the last crucial laps of the $2^1/_2$-mile track—unexpected mechanical problems or crashes (sometimes fatal) before the end of the race. Foyt's first victory, in 1961, was one of the most thrilling finishes in Indy history. Alternating the lead with Eddie Sachs (who would lose his life at the track in 1964) throughout the race, A.J. at last gained seconds of precious time as Sachs—with only three laps remaining—unexpectedly went to his pit for a tire change. As his competitor reentered the track from the straightaway, Foyt thundered past him and, while the spectators rose to their feet screaming and cheering, he flashed under the checkered flag. From that day forward, A. J. Foyt has dominated auto racing.

A driver of all kinds of automobiles, Foyt believes that nothing compares to driving "Indy-type" cars. "It takes precision to run in a circle," he has said, "and you're always on edge. There's always somebody breathing down your neck." He speaks of big-car racing as "the toughest test for drivers by far . . . it wears you down to a nub. It's like running a foot race. When you feel you're done in, you find you still have a mile to go."

The average speed of Foyt's 1964 Indy victory was 147.350 mph. Thirteen years later he became the only driver to score four victories there. No one may ever equal Foyt's record number of victories in more kinds of races, on more kinds of tracks, in more kinds of cars, than any driver in racing history. By 1980 he had to his credit (in the United States Auto Club competition) sixty-six victories in championship cars, forty-one in stock cars, twenty-eight in sprint cars, and twenty in midget cars. In 1968 he had won one stock-car crown to go with five championship car crowns, and in 1979 he won a second. In 1972 he won the new USAC dirt car division.

Either in racing or in the business of racing (he has engaged in several car-related business ventures), Foyt's goal continues to be first place. "I love racing," he says. "I couldn't ask for anything more from a sport. I've won everything there is to win but I still enjoy it." Physically, temperamentally, and professionally, Foyt is what racing is all about.

RICHARD PETTY (b. 1937)

Richard Petty—"King Richard," as he is called on the racing circuit—is the undisputed champion of the hell-for-leather sport of stock-car racing. Now in his forties, tall, lanky, curly-haired, and still heavy-footed, Petty has piled up 192 victories in twenty-two years of racing on the Grand National circuit. "When I put the hammer down," Petty has said, "some of those drivers just scatter. They think 'uh, oh, here comes No. 43.' "

Petty attributes his success as a driver to his ability to work well with a team. In his opinion, it is the combination of driver, car, and crew that produces the results. His crew is a family-synchronized operation any racer would envy. The Petty family dynasty goes back to the late 1940s, when Richard's father, Lee, raced as a hobby. Entering stock-car racing at the age of thirty-five, Lee Petty accumulated fifty-four victories, a record that has since been excelled only by his son and three other drivers. Father and son often raced in the same events, while Richard's brother Maurice—who is as devoted to building power-ful engines as Richard and Lee are to driving them—tends the mechanical end of the Petty stock-car company. The enterprise produces $1,000,000 a year in winnings and sponsorship money. "We've gone and done pretty good for ourselves," the King has commented, "and we've had a darned good time doing it."

The Petty family career has centered at the Daytona International Speedway. Lee Petty won the first Daytona 500 in 1959, and it was there, in the following year, that young Richard first beat his father in that event. (Father and son placed fourth and third.) After a severe accident in 1961, Lee Petty took over the management of the family team from the pits, and Richard became the star driver. In 1974 he ranked as the only four-time winner of the Daytona 500 (1964, 1966, 1971, and 1974).

After two decades, and more than 825 races later, Richard Petty has a winning record of nearly one in four races, and has made more than $3,500,000 in prize money. Said he about the exhausting business of driving his nearly 650-horsepower cars: "There's never any time to relax, because if you do you're going to wind up in the hospital." Unworried that, due to scarce fuel and sponsorship interest, the days of the powerful V-8 engine may be numbered, Petty is philosophical: "When there are no more V-8's, we'll race with V-6's, and when they are all gone we'll race with four cylinder jobs. We'll just keep going until it ain't no fun anymore."

◀ *Richard Petty, king of stock-car drivers,* James Drake, Photograph, 1979, Sports Illustrated

Robert Tyre Jones, Jr., Winning the British Open Golf Championship,
J. W. Williamson, for Currier & Ives, Lithograph, 1930,
United States Golf Association, Far Hills, New Jersey

GOLF

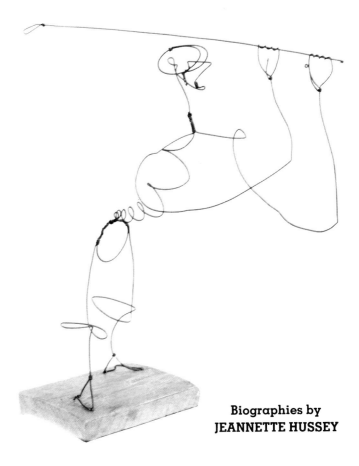

Golfer, Alexander Calder,
Wire sculpture,
Private collection

Biographies by
JEANNETTE HUSSEY

Right:
Francis Ouimet, Thomas E.
Stevens, Oil on canvas, c. 1954,
United States Golf Association,
Far Hills, New Jersey

Far right:
*Ouimet carried on the shoulders
of his fans after his victory at the
1913 U.S. Open,* The Francis
Ouimet Caddie Scholarship
Fund, Inc.

FRANCIS OUIMET (1893–1967)

America's love affair with golf began in 1913, at the United States Open, when Francis
Ouimet, an obscure twenty-year-old ex-caddie of very modest background, defeated two
celebrated British golfers—Harry Vardon and Ted Ray—in a stunning play-off at Brookline,
Massachusetts. The effect was electric. A nobody had become the first American to win the
U.S. Open. His triumph rocked the sports world, and in America transformed the
aristocratic game of golf into a sport for everyman.

Before World War I, Americans did not rank among the top international golfers.
Scottish, French, and British players dominated the game until Ouimet's victory at the
Country Club in Brookline. The London *Times* golf editor recalled the din on the fairway
that drizzly September day: "Tenors, basses, and baritones shouted themselves hoarse
through megaphones. Rope men worked like tigers. To hear the crowd thundering behind
gave one a realistic, alarming feeling of leading a cavalry charge." Then a "shout of triumph
as Francis holes a long and curly putt at the seventeenth, the putt which made certain the
most momentous win in all golfing history." The final score: Ouimet 72, Vardon 77, and
Ray 78.

Francis Ouimet almost literally grew up on the golf course. When he was seven, his
family settled in a house bordering the Country Club in Brookline. Later he attributed his
early interest in the game to his proximity, traversing the fairways on his way to school and,
at the age of eleven, becoming a "caddie-boy" like his elder brother. He carefully noticed

the successful plays of exceptional golfers and then imitated them on a homemade course the brothers had built in a cow pasture behind their house. "They say practice makes perfect," wrote Ouimet, "and I believe it."

After several failures to qualify for entry into the U.S. Amateur, Ouimet entered and won the Massachusetts Amateur in 1913. That year—while once again attempting to qualify for the national championship—he lost to defending champion Jerry Travers. It was a match that he said "did more toward getting me into the proper frame of mind than any I had ever had. I had been inclined," wrote this dedicated golfer, "to look upon golf lightly."

Yet Ouimet remained an amateur golfer, refusing ever to play the game for anything but pleasure. After his spectacular success in 1913, he twice won his major goal, the U.S. Amateur championship (1914, 1931). His record includes the French Amateur championship (1914) as well. Beginning in 1922 he was a member of the U.S. Walker Cup team, serving as its captain from 1936 to 1949. Although he shunned public attention, Ouimet was one of the most popular and respected figures in the game. Bobby Jones thought that he had "a God-given ability" to play golf. "I have often considered myself fortunate," Jones said, "to have been able to play with him, fortunate to have known him and very fortunate, indeed, to have occasionally beaten him in matches. There was no finer man." In 1951 Francis Ouimet received the ultimate accolade as the first non-Briton ever to be elected captain of the Royal and Ancient Golf Club of St. Andrews, Scotland, where the sport had been born.

Robert Tyre Jones, Jr., Thomas E. Stevens, Oil on canvas, 1953, United States Golf Association, Far Hills, New Jersey

BOBBY JONES (1902–1971)

"My first golf strokes were very short ones," wrote Bobby Jones, "even for a six-year-old." Jones grew up on a golf course—East Lake in Atlanta—where he "kept on hammering at the pesky ball until I found a way to make it behave." At age nine he was winning junior championships, and three years later a note on the clubhouse door read: "Bob Jones, Jr., age twelve, today shot a 70, tying the course record."

One decade after Francis Ouimet had started the golf ball rolling in America, his greatest successor set the pattern for American domination in the game. In 1923, Bobby Jones won the first of thirteen major golf titles. He ended in 1930, with the Grand Slam— four championships then consisting of both the Open and the Amateur titles in the United States and Great Britain.

In those eight perfect years, which had followed seven so lean that he had once threatened to quit golf, Jones played rounds that one writer called "incredible and indecent." A 1927 article described his flawless swing: "They wound up the Mechanical Man of Golf yesterday, and sent him clicking around the East Lake Course." "The 'Mechanical Man' stuff made me laugh," Jones wrote. "I have always said that I won golf tournaments because I tried harder than anyone else and was willing to take more punishment than the others." Into the Grand Slam, Jones said, he had put "all the knowledge, skill, resourcefulness and character of the first twenty years of my life."

Bobby Jones had all the makings of a popular idol. Blessed with clean good looks and elegant manners, he was the very image of the all-American boy as gentleman and sports hero. "Our Bobby" drew crowds wherever he went and sent thousands of duffers to the public links determined to copy the famous Jones stance. He was, wrote an admirer, "a singular star in a decade that had a galaxy of them." In June of 1930 New York City prepared a tickertape parade for Jones, just home in triumph after taking the British Amateur and the British Open championships. Jones later told a story about a friend who found himself in the Battery when the parade was forthcoming. The friend "approached one of New York's Finest . . . and asked what the parade was for. 'Oh,' said the policeman in obvious disgust, 'for some damned golf player.' "

Jones founded the annual Masters Tournament in Augusta, Georgia, in 1934, and he made a yearly appearance at the event. "Just walking around watching a match," Ben Hogan commented, "he's still the best attraction in golf." Later, a crippling spinal disease prevented Jones's attendance. Golf historian Herbert Warren Wind described Bobby Jones's strength of character: "As a young man he was able to stand up to just about the best that life can offer, which isn't easy, and later he stood up with equal grace to just about the worst."

141

Multiple-flash photo of Jones with a driver, Edgerton, Germeshausen and Grier, Photograph, Library of Congress

*Patty Berg, with the
Ladies Professional Golf
Association trophy,*
United Press International

PATTY BERG (b. 1918)

A pert, freckle-faced seventeen-year-old, often casually dressed in the same old sweater, slacks, and blue beret that seemed to bring her luck in tournaments, Patty Berg in 1935 was a "new kid on the block" among golfers. But that year she made golf headlines at the Interlachen Country Club, near her home in Minneapolis, by nearly defeating Glenna Collett Vare, the six-time winner of the National Amateur title who had dominated American women's golf since 1922. Stunned by the power and force of her game, sportscasters rightly predicted that Berg would become America's foremost woman golfer. Three years later she took the National Amateur championship and was selected by the Associated Press as the outstanding athlete of the year. By 1940 she had won every important American women's golf title.

As a pioneer among women pro golfers and a super-promoter of golf clinics and exhibitions, Berg has been, for forty years, one of the prime movers and shapers of golf in America. Described as a "natural" athlete, she included among her girlhood sports baseball, track, and football (she played quarterback on a local boys' team). One of a family of

Berg's organizational skills and Babe Didrikson's showmanship combined to establish women's professional golf, United Press International

championship golfers, she learned the game from her father, who also launched her on a series of exhibition tours, locally and in the West. The experience prepared her for a career, beginning in 1940 with the Wilson Sporting Goods Company. Sponsored by Wilson, she conducted golf clinics and exhibitions nationwide, and soon became golf's "goodwill ambassador," winning thousands of converts to the game. Berg's message was that nothing was impossible. "Too many people have the *wish* to win," she said, "when what they really need is the *will* to win."

One of the original organizers of the Ladies Professional Golf Association in 1948, Patty Berg served for four years as its first president. Three times during the 1950s, she was the leading money-winner on the tour, and in 1951 she was named a member of the LPGA's Hall of Fame. "I'm very happy I gave up football," she said at her induction ceremony, "or I wouldn't be here tonight."

Ben Hogan, Floyd Bright, Photograph, 1955, Sports Illustrated

BEN HOGAN (b. 1912)

"There is no such . . . individual as a born golfer," Ben Hogan told readers of his *Power Golf* (1948). Some may have more natural ability, but "they've all been made." Few were better made than Hogan himself. Admirers praised his capacity for intense concentration, his insatiable "appetite" for practicing, his "amazing, grim tenacity." Among his rivals—Byron Nelson, Jimmy Demaret, or Sam Snead of the "fluid, flawless, smooth, strong swing"—none dedicated himself so totally to the game.

"There he is moving up to his approach shot," Herbert Warren Wind wrote about Hogan at work,

> walking with that little waggle, his eyes fixed straight ahead. . . . the mouth set . . . in that locked grin, which should never be mistaken for a sign of Ben's enjoyment of the morning air, the devotion of his gallery, or the shot just played, however "right" it may have been. . . . After he plays a poor shot at a stage of a tournament when it might be costly, there is a change of expression. The grin becomes ironical and his cold, grey-blue eyes widen until they seem to be a full inch in height, and when you look at this man, so furious with himself, he is, as his colleagues refer to him, "The Hawk."

Unlike Francis Ouimet and Bobby Jones before him, Hogan missed some of the early advantages common to the game's superstars. No golf course graced the outskirts of Dublin, Texas, the small town where he was born; nor was his father (a blacksmith and mechanic) a golfer; nor did Hogan later—after his father had died and the family had moved to Fort Worth—impress the members of the Glen Garden Club, where he caddied, as a promising young golfer. His first contact with the game had come when he discovered, at the age of twelve, that caddying at Glen Garden paid more than peddling newspapers.

But at fifteen he surprised everyone when he tied for first place with another caddie, Byron Nelson, in the annual Christmas Day tournament. Despite a troublesome left hook, Hogan continued to enter amateur contests, and at nineteen—hoping to make golf his career—he turned professional. After an unimpressive career as an amateur and a few years on the pro circuit, Hogan broke into winning golf in 1940. He was then twenty-eight, the age when—ten years earlier—Bobby Jones had retired.

World War II interrupted Hogan's career, however, just as he had hit his stride in the early 1940s. He served three years in the Army Air Corps, and immediately returned to the pro circuit. Within five years (1948–53), Hogan took eight major championship titles: four U.S. Opens, two Masters, the PGA, and the British Open. It was a record even more outstanding when one considered that Hogan spent one of those years (1949) recuperating from a nearfatal automobile accident that left his golfing future seriously in doubt—to everyone but himself. While recovering from operations that jeopardized his ability even to walk normally again, he sent in his entry for the 1949 U.S. Open, with a note: "This may be just a dream, but miracles sometimes happen, and . . ." A year later he was back on the pro circuit.

The "Age of Hogan" coincided with a national golf boom. Having just emerged from a long war and a longer depression, Americans in mid-century were ready for a game with golf's appealing characteristics: a participant sport, available to all ages, either sex, or any degree of athletic ability. "If you have the keenness and determination," Hogan wrote in his introduction to *Power Golf*, "there isn't anything you can't accomplish in this game."

Palmer considered the winning of this Master's trophy the most satisfying event of his career, The National Museum of American History, Smithsonian Institution

Arnold Palmer,
Hy Peskin, Photograph,
1962, Sports Illustrated

ARNOLD PALMER (b. 1929)

Spectators demand miracles in sports, and during the 1960s Arnold Palmer was the "miracle maker." With his bold, "go for broke" surges down the stretch holes as he repeatedly turned defeat into victory, Palmer, in 1960, ushered in a new age of golf. Twice in that golden year, he rallied to win major championship titles—the Masters and the U.S. Open—and "when his putts fell into the hole," wrote one sports observer, "he laughed heartily and tossed his visor . . . into the breeze, and his happiness raced like electricity through the great throngs of people who followed him." "Arnie's Army," as they were called, became the most famous phenomenon in modern golf and, under television's ubiquitous eye, Palmer became the most popular and the richest champion that golf had ever known. To no one's surprise, in 1970 he was named athlete of the decade.

From the age of three, Arnold Daniel Palmer regularly rode a tractor around the golf course at Latrobe (Pennsylvania) Country Club with his father, Wilfred ("Deacon") Palmer, who was the club pro and always Arnold's best teacher and critic. "He never thought I hit the ball hard enough," Palmer once remarked. At five, young Arnold was swinging a cut-down ladies' iron and, at twenty-five, he won the U.S. Amateur, his first national title. By that time Palmer knew that he wanted to share in the excitement of the "eighteen-ring circus."

In *Go for Broke* (1973), a book about his philosophy of golf, Palmer described the abrupt change in his "whole spirit" and "entire attitude" concerning golf. It occurred in 1960 during the fourth, and last, round of the U.S. Open tournament at Cherry Hills (Denver). There, after three eighteen-hole rounds, he trailed in fifteenth place—"no more in contention," wrote one reporter, "than the man operating the hot dog concession." But a bold play on the troublesome first hole gave him a birdie—one stroke under par for the hole—and a new approach to golf. Suddenly he was struck by the way "boldness might influence not just a hole but an entire round, an entire tournament, and even an entire golfing career." Then, in one of golf's most amazing spurts under pressure, he birdied six of the next seven holes and won the championship with a seventy-two-hole score of 280. That charge became "a sort of phenomenon that marked my career," Palmer wrote. "I wasn't going to lead a life of dear-and-near misses."

For a decade, said his friend Mark McCormack, Palmer was excessively "written about, photographed, televised, filmed, exhibited, advertised, promoted." He was the first to exceed $1,000,000 in career winnings and, combined with related enterprises, his yearly income soon rose beyond that sum. Still, says he, "My chief aim is to be the best golfer in the world." He hopes, but so far has failed, to make the "Grand Slam" but, among his countless achievements, Palmer includes all of golf's major victories: the U.S. Amateur, the U.S. Open, the Masters (four times), and the British Open (twice).

Whether he wins or loses, the fans adore the way Arnie attacks the golf course. Sometimes thirty thousand strong, they crowd the greens and fairways to whoop and cheer and to distract Palmer's playing companions. Palmer, said a fellow player, "had only to hitch his trousers and prepare to meet the challenge and the gallery was transported. His emotions —pain, pleasure, dismay, anger and the rest—were never hidden, and his followers could relive through him their own joys and frustrations."

Jack Nicklaus: The Deadly Stroke, Donald Moss for Sports Illustrated, Acrylic and oil on canvas, Collection of the artist

JACK NICKLAUS (b. 1940)

All other golf records pale in comparison to Jack Nicklaus's achievements: eighteen major titles and, in 1980, still counting. He is the only golfer in history to win all four major tournaments—the Masters, the U.S. Open, the British Open, and the PGA championship—at least three times. Nicklaus "compels attention by performance alone," wrote P. J. Ward-Thomas, golf correspondent for the Manchester *Guardian*. "There is in him the stuff of the fantastic, the phenomenal, the likes of which may never be seen again. Clearly Nicklaus is—and will be—'the man to beat.' "

Unlike his predecessors, Jack Nicklaus did not *dream* of becoming a champion—he simply *was* one. That astonishing record of success came to him more easily than to any golfer in history. Growing up in Columbus, Ohio, he was encouraged in sports by his father, a pharmacist and himself a first-rate athlete. "He once said I was too chubby to run track," Jack recalled. "So I went out and won three races. . . . My folks still like to chide me," he added, "that I can't win a certain tournament. It makes me try harder, I suppose."

Jack excelled in baseball and basketball and, in his first game of golf at the age of ten, he shot a 51 for nine holes. As a beginner in golf, he was instructed to hit the ball as hard as he could and to worry about style later. Having qualified for the National Amateur championship at age fifteen, he was considered a child prodigy, and by 1959 he was good enough to win the U.S. Amateur. His second National Amateur victory was described as "so commanding, so ruthless, and so assured it seemed preordained." At this point, only Arnold Palmer was his superior. In December 1961, Nicklaus decided to make golf his career, and he determined to win the 1962 Open.

Palmer was at the top of his career that summer when the two men met for the U.S. Open title at the Oakmont (Pennsylvania) Country Club. After seventy-two holes the score was tied, and Nicklaus found himself pitted against the national hero and his entire hostile "army" for an eighteen-hole showdown. But neither screaming legions nor Palmer's hell-for-leather charge shattered Jack's superb ability to concentrate—his greatest single asset. "I never got scared," he calmly commented. "I told myself to keep playing my own game—and I did." Having won by three strokes, he became (at twenty-two) the youngest golfer to capture the U.S. Open title.

Nicklaus's massive power and accuracy were indisputable. The velocity of his tee shots has been compared to shell fire, and his putts described as having the delicacy of a diamond cutter. One admirer considered the quality of "impregnable confidence"—Jack Nicklaus's belief in himself—to be at the core of his game. In the last eighteen years he has won five Masters tournaments, three British Opens, four PGA championships, and, in June 1980, shooting better than ever at the age of forty, he took his fourth U.S. Open title. One seasoned spectator called Nicklaus's performance "sporting theater at its finest." Said *Sports Illustrated:* "It also closed the door on the question, who's the greatest golfer ever."

Tennis at Newport, George Bellows, Oil on canvas, 1920, Mr. and Mrs. Barron U. Kidd

BILL TILDEN (1893-1953)

"Big Bill" Tilden's elegant full-court play highlighted the Golden Age of Tennis in the 1920s. A slender 6'2", he wore the traditional white tennis flannels with a Main Line Philadelphia grace. His first big championship—Wimbledon in 1920—wasn't won until he was twenty-seven, but it signaled his coronation as the King of Tennis. Big Bill Tilden would dominate the center court as much as the Sultan of Swat or the Manassa Mauler dominated baseball and boxing in the same era.

But Tilden would always be a more aloof figure, a more complicated personality than many American sports heroes. A looming presence on the courts, he played at times with such nonchalance that the galleries jeered. Tilden fed on this kind of hostility, and often played his best amid the catcalls. He was a consummate sportsman. If a controversial call was made against him, he acted with grace; if a bad call was made against his opponent, Tilden would inevitably throw the next point in a supreme gesture of fairness.

Almost single-handedly, Tilden transformed tennis from an elitist pastime to a popular sport. Tennis had taken root in the United States on the grass courts of privilege in the 1870s and 1880s. The United States Lawn Tennis Association (USLTA) was founded in 1880 to promote courtly competition, and the U.S. championships were fought for the first time on Newport's meticulously cultivated turf courts in 1881. Newport immediately became a fixture of the social season, but the patronage of the Four Hundred made it an exclusive enclave. No other significant tennis tournaments were played in America until the West Side Tennis Club of Forest Hills, Long Island, insinuated itself into the inner circle of tennis in 1915. While not exactly democratizing the sport, Forest Hills at least broadened tennis's popularity by widening the field of competition and making it accessible to some who couldn't fit into Mrs. Astor's ballroom. And, when sports in general burst into a Golden Age in the 1920s, tennis found its métier. The glamour and elegant excitement of the game epitomized the glitter of the age and, because it was a game which focused on individual play, the time was ripe for the sport to produce a true national hero. Into this beckoning spotlight stepped Big Bill Tilden, whose impeccable social credentials and winning public personality helped make him America's first tennis superstar.

Tilden won the U.S. National crown seven times, and for ten years was considered the number-one tennis player in the world. He won seventy tennis titles in America and around the world, achieving great popularity in France, Italy, Austria, Switzerland, Britain, and Australia. From 1920 to 1930, he won seventeen challenge matches in Davis Cup competition, and he won at Wimbledon in 1920, 1921, and 1930. He turned professional in 1931, and played in tournaments well into his fifties.

Along the way, Tilden also dabbled in the theater—which he always called his first love—and wrote some forgettable fiction and drama. He never distinguished himself in the arts and remained a frustrated Shakespearean actor all his life, but celebrity suited him. He lived in Hollywood and was a familiar figure at parties and poolside, mixing easily with the new stars of the silver screen. But Tilden never left the tennis circuit. When he went on tour, he used the center court as a stage, playing under the lights and enrapturing crowds with one-night "shows," from Madison Square Garden to the big indoor arenas of the West Coast. In his memoirs he wrote that, before his time, tennis had been played "with an air of elegance—a peculiar courtly grace that seemed to rob the game of its thrills." What he did, as he said, was to give the game "something more vital and fundamental." What he brought to it was a showmanship that became an integral part of tennis.

In June 1953, at the age of sixty, Tilden died of a heart attack in his Hollywood apartment while packing his bags for a tournament in Cleveland. Only two years before, the Associated Press had listed him among the greatest athletes of the first half of the century, and in 1969 an international panel of tennis writers named Tilden the greatest player of all time.

◄ *Bill Tilden,* Frederick Lewis Collection, New York

Helen Wills, Miguel Covarrubias, Tempera on bristol board, c. 1927, Humanities Research Center, University of Texas at Austin

Helen Wills Moody, Enid Foster, Bronze, 1924, Mr. and Mrs. Albert Ritzenberg

TENNIS

Biographies by
AMY HENDERSON

HELEN WILLS (b. 1905)

Queen of American tennis in the 1920s, Helen Wills—dubbed "Little Miss Poker Face" by the press—was known for her dispassionate public personality and her grinding dispatch of opponents. Seemingly unflappable, she once said, "When I play, I become entirely absorbed in the game. I love the feel of hitting the ball hard." She became the sports darling of the media through sheer brute force. "She is powerful, repressed and imperturbable," wrote the New York *Herald Tribune*. "She plays her game with a silent, deadly earnestness, concentrated on her work. That, of course, is the way to win games, but it does not please galleries. Of course, there is no reason why an amateur athlete should try to please galleries." Because Wills never played to the crowds, she never won the kind of open adulation accorded Big Bill Tilden. Yet she mesmerized audiences with her steely determination. If she was not warmly embraced by the crowds, she was unquestionably respected as an awesome presence, a kind of indomitable force.

Wills represented a type of women's tennis player not seen before. In a decade that cheered flamboyance, she possessed none of the flapper's frivolity. However charming and social she proved off court, there was nothing sweet or vulnerable about her from the baseline. Intensely serious and self-controlled on the court, Wills blasted her opponents into submission with blazing shots from all angles. She was the first American woman to play an all-around tennis game, with sound net and backcourt play and good basic strokes. She didn't leap balletically across the court; she ran. She even sweated. Coolly. What she gave women's tennis was a vitality it had never had before.

She also changed the style of women's court dress in America, tossing out the traditional long, heavy skirt and corset for the middy blouse, mid-calf-length skirt, and her trademark green-lined eyeshade. These changes, both stylistic and substantive, were revolutionary, and heralded the fifty-year fight to make women's tennis a true competition sport rather than a decorative sideshow.

For ten years, beginning in 1923 when she was seventeen, Helen Wills was the dominant figure in American women's tennis, winning seven U.S. championships and eight Wimbledon titles. One of her longest and most publicized rivalries was with Helen Jacobs, a younger and perhaps more talented player with whom she had often been matched since their California childhoods. Their rivalry reached a climax in the 1930s. Wills—now Mrs. Frederick Moody —had passed up the National championships in 1932, and Helen Jacobs had won. The next year, however, the two met in the finals at Forest Hills. They split the first two sets when, with Jacobs leading in the third, Helen Wills Moody suddenly walked to the umpire's chair and withdrew from the contest. The crowd was stunned, and there was outrage that the match had not been played out. Mrs. Moody explained that she had become dizzy with pain from a back injury. "Had I been able to think clearly," she later wrote, "I might have chosen to remain. Animals and humans, however, prefer to suffer in a quiet, dark place."

She didn't play again until Wimbledon in 1935, where once more she faced Helen Jacobs in the finals. The "Battle of the Two Helens" was one of the greatest matches in tennis history, and when Helen Wills Moody won—6-3, 3-6, 7-5—Little Miss Poker Face let out an uncharacteristic whoop and threw her racquet high into the air in triumph. She then retired, only to make a final comeback appearance at Wimbledon in 1938, where she once again beat Helen Jacobs, this time 6-4, 6-0. With that, she left competitive tennis forever.

DON BUDGE (b. 1915)

In the wake of dismal performances at the U.S. Singles championship at Forest Hills in 1935, *Time* magazine bewailed the passing of tennis's Golden Age: "For people who cling patriotically to the myth of U.S. supremacy in sport, the game of tennis has lately been a painful disappointment." The only bright spot seemed to be the play of Don Budge—"The California Comet"—who burst upon the national tennis scene that year at the age of twenty and was heralded as having "the potentialities of a world champion." He had learned to play tennis when he was eight years old, and at eighteen this "diffident, stringy, surprisingly agile youth," as described by one sportswriter, had won the California men's title. Budge, who had learned to play not at country clubs but on public courts, was called the "archetype of the thousands of prodigious youngsters who since the [First World] War have taken U.S. tennis away from Society."

Selected for the Davis Cup team in 1935, he did better than any other American in the preliminary rounds. Budge made his Wimbledon debut that year as well and, though he failed to win, he established himself as an immediate crowd favorite when, stepping onto the courts, he greeted Queen Mary in the royal box with a cheerful wave of his racquet instead of the usual formal bow—and got a cheerful wave in return. Two years later he would return to Wimbledon and win everything in sight, including the men's singles, men's doubles, and mixed doubles titles. By 1937 his smashing style of attack and wicked two-handed backhand were literally unbeatable. An opponent said that playing against Budge was "like playing against a concrete wall."

Shortly after his win at Wimbledon in 1937, Don Budge met his chief rival—Germany's Baron Gottfried Von Cramm—at the Davis Cup singles finals in a match that has been called the greatest ever played. Just before the match began, Von Cramm was called to the phone. He later told Budge that "it was Hitler. He wanted to wish me good luck." According to Budge, Von Cramm came out "pale and serious and played as if his life depended on every point." In five sets of perfect tennis, not a soft shot was made by either player. London papers called it "an exhilarating display of two great tennis machines," and "not so much a contest as a cumulative spectacle."

The fifth, and final, set began at 7:30 p.m., and the score went to 6-6 with Budge serving. He won the advantage only to have the Baron come back to deuce. "The crowd was so quiet," Budge recalled, "I am sure they could hear us breathing." On the sixth match point, the rally was prolonged. Von Cramm hit a forehand cross court, and—in what has been called the shot of the century—Budge lunged in desperation. Sprawled on all fours, he "realized the ball felt pretty good on the racquet. I looked up in time to see Von Cramm try to reach it on his right-hand side and miss it." When the match ended in semidarkness at 8:45 p.m., Budge had won—6-8, 5-7, 6-4, 6-2, 8-6—and the Americans had won their first Davis Cup since 1926. For his efforts, Budge was subsequently awarded the Sullivan trophy as America's outstanding amateur athlete of 1937.

In 1938, the affable redhead accomplished the "Grand Slam" of tennis by winning the U.S., British, French, and Australian singles titles—something that not even Big Bill Tilden had ever done. That fall, having won everything amateur tennis had to offer, Budge turned professional, making his debut before a rhapsodic crowd of sixteen thousand at Madison Square Garden in January 1939. He continued to play regularly in professional tournaments until the mid-1950s.

◀ *Don Budge shown here at Wimbledon in 1938, the year in which he swept all the major amateur titles,* Keystone Press Agency, Inc.

Jack Kramer, United
States Tennis Association

JACK KRAMER (b. 1921)

With his courtly Golden Age grace, Bill Tilden had transformed tennis into a popular
American sport in the 1920s, but it took another generation of players to change the style
of the sport itself. In the late 1940s, Jack Kramer did just that, tearing tennis from its classic
roots and throwing it into a modern Circus Maximus known as the "Big Game." Explosive
serve-and-volley rallies and net smashes replaced the slower baseline-to-baseline game of
elegant lobs. White flannels were exchanged for T-shirts and shorts, and, where players had
once concentrated on form as much as on a successful shot, they now seemed more intent
on charging the net. Kramer's power game became the New Tennis, and the crowds loved
it.

Who was this Visigoth? A blond, strapping youth from California with an easy grin who
liked to call himself "Big Jake," Jack Kramer had won the National Boys Singles and
Doubles championships at the age of fourteen. At seventeen, he became the youngest player
ever to represent America in a Davis Cup challenge round. Then, with the advent of World
War II, he served in the Coast Guard before resuming his tennis career seriously in 1946.
From 1946 through 1954, Jack Kramer honed the power game which would make him the
world's strongest player. Although a badly blistered hand and tennis elbow contributed to
his defeat at Wimbledon in the summer of 1946, he was nevertheless hailed at that tournament as "having the greatest mastery of strokes and the keenest lawn tennis brain" of
any player there. Later in the season, he captured the U.S. National championship at
Forest Hills and then, chosen to represent America again in Davis Cup competition, helped
win the Cup back from Australia.

By 1947—a year in which Kramer successfully defended the Davis Cup—he had won his first and only Wimbledon, and captured the National Indoor Singles championship as well as retaining his U.S. Singles title at Forest Hills. Kramer's incredibly powerful serve and cannon-like forehand became the game's standards. *Time* wrote that he "plays tennis the way Joe Louis stalks an opponent in the ring. He is always boring in, always making the other fellow feel he is doomed unless he does something tremendous."

Kramer radiated confidence. "When a guy runs up a lead on me, I'm surprised," he said. "I think he's either playing over his head or lucky." He characterized his serve-and-volley game as "no defense"—a calculation of the sport so precise that a player could place a shot and virtually know in advance how his opponent would return it. The percentage came in holding your serve and waiting for your opponent to make an error. "There is no time to think on a tennis court," Kramer explained, so "the less you think the better off you are."

In October of 1947, with no real competition looming in amateur circles, Kramer turned professional, touring the 1947–48 season with Bobby Riggs and earning $50,000. He beat Riggs sixty-nine matches to twenty that year, and went on, in subsequent seasons, to annihilate Pancho Gonzales (96–27) and Pancho Segura (64–28). Riggs called Kramer "a merciless competitor. Even when he had huge leads in our series, Jack was sore when he lost. He fought from the first match to the last."

Kramer retired in 1954, but soon proved as crafty a professional tennis promoter and businessman as he had a player. Throughout the 1950s and 1960s, he was often a controversial figure, especially when raiding amateur ranks to stock his professional tourneys with players. More important, he was to prove a leading force in the ultimate modernization of the sport, the opening of tournaments to both amateur and professional players.

The eighteen-year-old Kramer in the National Men's Singles, Chicago, 1939, United Press International

PANCHO GONZALES (b. 1928)

Pancho Gonzales began his tennis career at the age of twelve, when his mother gave him a fifty-cent racquet to keep him from playing "rough games like football, where he might get hurt." He never took lessons—"and I never will"—but learned by watching other players. And, when he was twenty, he came from virtually nowhere to win the U.S. championships at Forest Hills.

Gonzales looked like a cheetah on the courts, prowling effortlessly and with a killer's instinct. Six-foot-three and a lithe 185 pounds, he had incredible reflexes and a blistering service—once clocked at 112 mph—that made the galleries gasp.

He created a sensation by winning that first championship at Forest Hills in 1948, but it was a year in which the reigning men's amateur titleholder—Ted Schroeder—had not played. As if to emphasize the flukishness of his win, Gonzales immediately lost his next half-dozen tournaments, earning the sobriquet "Gorgo"—short for Gorgonzola—for being "the greatest cheese champion in American tennis history." In 1949, however, he met and defeated Schroeder in the finals at Forest Hills, 16–18, 2–6, 6–1, 6–2, 6–4. Shortly thereafter, he turned professional, joining up to tour with Jack Kramer for $80,000, but playing so badly that first year that he was dropped as Kramer's partner. He didn't reemerge as a force on the pro circuit again until 1954 and 1955, when he played brilliantly and won recognition finally as the best tennis player in the world. He reigned for the next eight years, winning out consistently over Ken Rosewall, Tony Trabert, Lew Hoad, and Pancho Segura.

Gonzales was an inconsistent player, sometimes indolent, sometimes driven. He never trained, smoked when he felt like it, and ate what he wanted. "If I lose a few matches," he once said, "I stop smoking, go to bed early, and pay more attention to what I eat. In a few days I'm all right again." This magic formula worked so well that, though he retired several times, he was still playing and still collecting prize money in the 1970s. One of Gonzales's most remarkable matches was his 1969 victory at Wimbledon when he was forty-one. In the longest match ever played there—five hours and twelve minutes—he beat twenty-five-year-old Charles Pasarell 22–24, 1–6, 16–14, 6–3, 11–9. He has been compared to "the aging Olivier on the stage or the aged Rubinstein at the piano," for "one comes away not merely pleased to have been in his company, but further instructed in the subtleties of an art."

A sportswriter wrote of Gonzales, in his prime, that "he has the same crowd appeal as the Babe [Ruth], the same wonderfully child-like enjoyment in his work, and to a degree the same devil-may-care attitude about the game."

◄ *Pancho Gonzales at Wimbledon in 1949,* Photoworld

Arthur Ashe, Jeanne Moutoussamy-Ashe,
Photograph, Collection of the photographer

*Ashe upsets Jimmy Connors in
the Wimbledon finals, 1975,* Tony Triolo,
Photograph, Sports Illustrated

ARTHUR ASHE (b. 1943)

The first time Arthur Ashe threw his racquet in anger, he was ten years old, and his father reached him before the racquet hit the ground. It was the last time he ever threw a tantrum on a tennis court. Ronald Charity, the man who initially got him interested in the game, saw young Arthur as a quiet, observant youth who took in everything. "He was very disciplined. The level of his game kept going up." Charity took him for training to Dr. Robert W. Johnson, a black physician and tennis enthusiast, in Lynchburg, Virginia. Ashe recalled that the sessions were rigorous, because Dr. Johnson "figured that in the segregated South at the time—early 1950s—if any of the tournament directors could figure out any excuses for kicking us black kids out, they would do it." So Johnson picked out "the kids who could take the mental pressure of not exploding on the court." The scholarly-looking Ashe developed into a controlled, taut player, seemingly imperturbable. It was small wonder that, at the height of his career, he would find the strut-and-pout exhibitionism of some of his colleagues "embarrassing."

In 1960 and 1961, Ashe won the U.S. Indoor Junior championship, the first time a black had captured a national men's tennis title. He went to the University of California at Los Angeles on a tennis scholarship, and there met the man he called his hero—Pancho Gonzales. "It was the greatest break of my life," he said. "Pancho not only was the best tennis player in the world but most people agree he had the sharpest tennis mind. He could look at you hit a ball once and diagnose all your mistakes." Gonzales taught Ashe the thundering service which had been his own trademark—and, in fact, taught him so well that he has said that the greatest tennis set he ever played was one he lost to Ashe.

Throughout the mid-1960s, Ashe continued to develop his game, and sportswriters began to call him "the most promising player in the world." In 1968, he seemed to hit the top. Surging on a twenty-match winning streak, Ashe came to the U.S. championships at Forest Hills and beat out all comers in this first American "open" tourney between amateurs and professionals. Playing Tom Okker in the finals, he used his 115-mph serve and a repertoire of seventeen different backhand shots to down "The Dutch Flyer."

At this stage in his career, Ashe played strictly a power game, concentrating on overwhelming opponents with the velocity of his shots. Yet, in the next several years, this style of play was to prove his downfall. His failure to create a more subtle game led many to call him a dazzling disappointment. But then, after his thirtieth birthday, Ashe found his stride. He worked hard at giving his game not only greater flexibility but more discipline and sophistication. By the 1975 Wimbledon, he had honed his skills to a coruscating sheen. His opponent for the title was his longtime antagonist, number-one-ranked Jimmy Connors. The final score was a stunning 6-1, 6-1, 5-7, 6-4, and Arthur Ashe was master of Wimbledon.

Less than two years later, he underwent surgery to remove a calcium deposit on his heel. Throughout 1977 and 1978, Ashe mercilessly worked himself back into shape. By early 1979, he was in the finals at the Masters and the U.S. Pro Indoor. In April 1979, *World Tennis* magazine proclaimed, "If you look at the whole picture, Ashe has been the most significant male tennis player of the open era." Three months later, the 6'1", 150-pound Ashe—a supremely conditioned athlete with a resting pulse rate of 52—had a heart attack at the age of thirty-six. He had recently been ranked seventh in the world, and his first thoughts after recovering were to return to the tour and "get myself back up to No. 7 by, say, next Easter. I've always been goal oriented, and for me that is a worthy goal. And I'm going to chase every ball." For a few months, it looked like he'd make it, but, after suffering recurrent heart trouble, Arthur Ashe left tournament tennis in 1980.

BILLIE JEAN KING (b. 1943)

"And now," the tournament announcer trumpets, "the working symbol for equal rights in America. . . . Mrs! . . . Billie! . . . Jean! . . . KING!!!!" Out she charges to center court, engulfed by the crowd's roar. Inextricably tied to the growth of women's tennis, Billie Jean King has symbolized the struggle for equality in sport for more than two decades.

The daughter of a California fireman, she first caught the tennis world's eye at Wimbledon in 1962 when, as an unknown, she almost toppled top-ranked Margaret Smith. Four years later, Billie Jean won the women's singles title at Wimbledon, as she would again five more times, along with four doubles titles and four in mixed doubles—a record twenty Wimbledon titles. She also won the U.S. championship at Forest Hills in 1967, 1971, 1972, and 1974. A friend has said that she was "the one who was able to channel everything into winning, into being the consummate tennis player."

In the late 1960s and early 1970s, she led the fight for women's tennis as the whole game was undergoing a metamorphosis from an amateur to a professional sport. In 1968, the amateur bastions of Forest Hills and Wimbledon opened their tournaments to professionals, and the professional ranks soon swelled. The professionalization of tennis was a pivotal moment in women's tennis, and Billie Jean King was in the forefront of those who sought to seize the moment.

Billie Jean King at Wimbledon, Gerry Cranham, Photograph, 1973, Sports Illustrated

King with Chris Evert, Tony Triolo, Photograph, 1975, Sports Illustrated

She helped organize the women's pro circuit, including the sixteen-club Women's Team Tennis. In the early 1970s, she and several others played in the Virginia Slims tournaments in open competition with the amateur circuit sponsored by the U.S. Lawn Tennis Association. Billie Jean resented the "damned country club" idea of tennis, which kept women on a lacy fringe, and she focused on money as the key to change. "Money is what people respect," she has said, "and when you are a professional athlete, they want to know how much you have made. They judge you on that." In 1971 she became the first woman athlete to earn $100,000 in a single year.

Ranked number one in the world four times, and in the U.S. seven times, between 1965 and 1973, she reached the media high point of her career in 1973, in her classic "Battle of the Sexes" duel with Bobby Riggs, the 1939 men's world champion. Riggs had recently drubbed Margaret Smith Court, taunting her into a humiliating defeat in a match played on Mother's Day. He next challenged Billie Jean, and they met at the Houston Astrodome on September 20, 1973. In a circus-like atmosphere, replete with a parade of hundreds of musicians and marchers dressed like elephants and gladiators, the largest crowd ever to witness a tennis match (30,472 at the Astrodome, and a television audience estimated at 50,000,000) watched as Billie Jean was carried to center court on an Egyptian litter, and Riggs in a rickshaw. He gave her an all-week caramel sucker, and she gave him a live baby pig (with pink bow) in honor of his status as chief male chauvinist. Despite the hoopla, the game itself was played with a grudge-match intensity. Billie Jean handily beat the chipmunk of superhype 6–4, 6–3, 6–3. Afterward she said: "This is the culmination of a lifetime in the sport. Tennis has always been reserved for the rich, the white, the males—and I've always been pledged to change all that."

National Junior Olympics, International Swimming Hall of Fame, Fort Lauderdale, August 1980,
Tim and Karen Morse, Photograph, Collection of the photographers

SWIMMING

Biographies by
JEANNETTE HUSSEY

Duke Kahanamoku at the 1920 Olympics, United Press International

Kahanamoku (c. 1923) tandem-surfing, a sport he pioneered,
Viola Cady Krahn

DUKE KAHANAMOKU (1890–1968)

Long before the mid-twentieth century, when the romance of surfing first touched the national imagination, Duke Kahanamoku regularly rode the waves at Waikiki Beach in Hawaii. "I was about eight years old when I started surfing," Kahanamoku recalled in 1967. "We had nobody to teach us how to ride the waves . . . we had to learn ourselves." Once the sport of Hawaiian royalty, surfing was banned by Calvinist missionaries who controlled the islands after 1820. At the turn of the century, it began to show signs of revival.

In 1908, Duke and his surfing friends organized in Honolulu one of the first amateur surfing clubs, Hui Nalu (Club of the Waves). Members gathered to discuss the condition of the surf and to formulate some of the rules still in use today. The surfer "matches his own skill and courage against a devastating display of the forces of nature," wrote one enthusiast, "and triumphantly challenges the ocean with his poise and confidence. . . . Just to have the courage to try is an accomplishment." The Duke's surfing skills were legends in his time. He pioneered tandem surfing (one surfer sitting on the shoulders of another) in 1919; he was the first to wind-surf (to use a sail attached to the surfboard), and the first to wake-surf (on the wake behind a motorboat). As a famous swimmer, Kahanamoku traveled abroad to teach water-safety methods for the Red Cross; and, wherever he traveled, Duke introduced his first love—surfing.

A Hawaiian representing the United States, Kahanamoku preceded Johnny Weissmuller as an Olympic swimming champion. He collected three gold and two silver medals in four Olympiads, and replaced the outmoded scissors kick with his novel flutter kick. Duke described his training in the early days as a "natural method. . . . I swam as far as I felt like and quit." At the age of forty-two, he was a member of the water polo team in the 1932 games. "I wanted to see if I could still swim," he said.

A tall, strong, and striking figure, Kahanamoku is said to have been of a royal Hawaiian lineage. He was elected sheriff of Honolulu—an office he held for thirty-six years—and presided at the same time as Hawaii's Ambassador-at-Large, the symbol of Polynesian charm. The New York *Times* described him as "Hawaii's best-known citizen."

Gertrude Ederle emerges from the surf following her 1926 Channel swim, Bettmann Archive, Inc.

Swimmingly Yours,
Gertrude Trudy Ederle
NEW YORK
Successful Channel Swim
Aug. 6, 1926
Cap Gris Nez to Kingsdown
14 HOURS 30 MIN.

GERTRUDE EDERLE (b. 1906)

Overnight, America's Gertrude Ederle became the most famous woman in the world after her record-breaking swim across the English Channel on August 6, 1926. The 5'5'', 125-pound Olympic medalist was only the sixth swimmer—the first woman—to succeed in conquering the Channel, and the first to have done so in less than sixteen hours. Ederle's time: 14 hours 31 minutes. "She was the demonstration of those times," Paul Gallico wrote, "that courage, training, willpower and indomitable spirit comprise the secret weapon against seemingly unconquerable obstacles . . . but she went through hell."

Strong tides, choppy waves, and icy water were the obstacles against which Ederle pitted her small frame when she entered the water at Cap Gris-Nez, France. Odds were 3 to 1 that she would fail—that she could not achieve her goal of reaching Dover, much less swim it in record time. Wearing layers of olive oil, lanolin, Vaseline, and lard, and accompanied by two tugs carrying relatives, newsmen, photographers, swimming coach, and other interested swimmers, Gertrude plunged in at 7:08 a.m. and began to cut her way through the water. A sign on the side of one tug read "This Way, Ole Kid!" with an arrow pointing forward.

With strong, "space-eating" crawl strokes, she pushed ahead. Urged to slow her pace, she refused, pausing only briefly to take food. Occasionally a member of the party would join her in the water to boost her spirits. But, by midafternoon, wind, rain, monstrous swells, and a cross-tide hampered progress and forced her to swim thirty-five miles to cover the twenty-one-mile distance. Refusing to give up—"What for?" she asked those who implored her to quit—she reached shallow water at Kingsdown on the Dover coast at 9:04 p.m.

The daughter of a New York delicatessen owner, "Trudy" Ederle had early in life shown outstanding physical stamina. She learned to swim at the age of six and, at fourteen, won her first big race—a three-mile swim against fifty top competitors in New York Bay. Within three years she held eighteen world's distance records. In 1924, at the Paris Olympiad, she won a gold medal as a member of the U.S. 400-meter relay team, and two bronze medals for third place in the 100-meter and 400-meter freestyle races. The following year, she bettered the men's record for the twenty-one-mile distance from the Battery in lower New York to Sandy Hook, New Jersey, in 7 hours 11 minutes.

Now, at nineteen, triumphant after her second attempt to swim the Channel, Ederle was the toast of New York. Given a monumental motorcade up lower Broadway, she was cheered by an adoring crowd straining to catch a glimpse of her, "her arms extended," wrote one observer, "as if to embrace them all." In a ceremony at City Hall, Mayor Jimmy Walker, epitomizing the exuberance of the 1920s, compared her achievement to Moses crossing the Red Sea, Caesar crossing the Rubicon, and Washington crossing the Delaware. Calvin Coolidge called her "America's best girl," and the *Saturday Evening Post* editorialized: "In all the annals of sport there is no finer record than that hung up by this young American girl."

Although misfortune—in the form of deafness and a spinal injury—prevented her from enjoying the limelight for long, Gertrude Ederle reflected philosophically about the fickleness of fame. "It doesn't matter if they've forgotten me. I haven't forgotten them," she said. "It was worth it."

New York welcomes Ederle following her Channel conquest, Bettmann Archive, Inc.

JOHNNY WEISSMULLER (b. 1904)

Swimming assumed the American spotlight in 1924, when Johnny Weissmuller starred in the Paris Olympic games, capturing three gold medals and gaining center stage for a decade of record-breaking achievements. At the Amsterdam games in 1928 he won two more golds, breaking his own records in the 100-meter and the 800-meter relay. No specialist in any one stroke or distance, Weissmuller was the total champion. He swam every event from 50 yards to the half-mile and, during ten years of amateur competition, he remained undefeated. His 100-yard freestyle record (51 seconds), set in 1927 without benefit of starting blocks, lane lines, or flip turns, stood for seventeen years. He took fifty-two national titles and set sixty-seven world records by 1928, when he retired. In 1950 he was voted "The Greatest Swimmer of the Half-Century" by 250 sportswriters and broadcasters of the Associated Press. He was "the great dramatizer of swimming," and it seemed as if he "had been deliberately invented and carpentered for the sport."

Raised in Chicago by poor, Viennese immigrant parents, Weissmuller recalled spending his "tadpole" days with his younger brother at the "Baby Beach" (Fullerton Beach) on the shore of Lake Michigan. Later he braved the deep, rough waters of "The Rocks" along the lake shore. At the age of fifteen, he demonstrated his "terrible stroke" to Bill Bachrach, coach of the Illinois Athletic Club, who drilled him in a year-long rigorous training program. He promptly broke four Amateur Athletic Union championship records and thereafter never lost a major race.

Weissmuller regarded Bachrach's lessons in relaxation as "the greatest secret" of his success. Observing Johnny strolling into line before the starter's gun at the 1924 Paris Olympics, Grantland Rice wrote that he "was about as tense as a loose towel." His cool, unruffled self-confidence aptly suited the strenuous tests of the champion. Then at his physical peak—6'3", 190 pounds, and superbly coordinated—Weissmuller possessed the classic frame for a swimmer: broad-shouldered, full-chested, with a slim, muscular torso. He was universally described by sportswriters as a handsome, poised Adonis. No challenger could touch him. He swam with a unique style—back arched, head and shoulders thrust full out of the water, elbows cocked high. His body seemed endowed with a special buoyancy described as "half human, half hydrofoil." Said Robert Kuphuth, the 1928 U.S. Olympic Team coach: "I've seen the most durable of athletes, Nurmi and Zatopek in track, Armstrong and Greb in boxing, Hogan in golf, Cobb in baseball. But I'd have to say Weissmuller had the most fantastic endurance of any champion."

Swimming turned out to be Weissmuller's passport from poverty to a unique place as a double legend among American sports and entertainment heroes. In 1930 he successfully made the transition from heroism as the greatest freestyle swimmer in the world to one of the best-known, best-loved Hollywood film stars. As Edgar Rice Burroughs's famous jungle hero, "Tarzan, the Ape Man," he made nineteen films. "It was up my alley," said Weissmuller about his Tarzan role. "There was swimming in it, and I didn't have much to say."

Johnny Weissmuller at the 1924 Olympics; he would compete ▶
in the 1928 Olympics to bring his total of gold medals
to five, United Press International

Mark Spitz, 1972,
Personality Posters,
Inc., New York

MARK SPITZ (b. 1950)

"The medals weighed a lot," said Mark Spitz about this pose. "They have heavy, crazy chains. Really, it was hard to stand up straight wearing them all at one time."

For the most popular poster ever made of an athlete, Spitz wore the seven gold medals he had won in swimming events at the 1972 Olympiad in Munich, West Germany. There, in a performance unsurpassed in sports history, he earned four golds in individual competition and three as a member of relay teams—all in world-record time.

"No Olympic star ever shone more brightly," wrote one observer of Spitz at Munich. At 6 feet, 170 pounds, slender, broad-shouldered, with slim hips, long arms, large hands, and unusually flexible legs, he possessed the perfect physique for a swimmer. He could "kick six inches deeper than anyone else. His legs," said teammate Jerry Heidenreich, "are like a bow." In his first event—the 200-meter butterfly in which he had finished last at Mexico City four years earlier—Spitz first conquered a mental block against that painful event, and then set a new world record: 2 minutes 7 seconds. Said he: "I feel like this is going to be just fine, now." He had won his first gold and, within the week, six others followed.

California-born, Spitz began formal swimming instruction in Sacramento at the age of eight. His father, a steel-company executive, was the driving force in his career. Before 1972 he had set twenty-three world records and thirty-five U.S. records. A major setback occurred at the Mexico City games in 1968, "the worst meet of my life," where he had not performed up to his own high expectations. Afterward he spent four years at Indiana University as a premed student and—as a member of the nation's foremost collegiate swimming team—he fell under the sound guidance of Coach Jim ("Doc") Counsilman. It was "like a comeback for me," said Spitz at the age of twenty. Counsilman considered him "one of the all-time great athletes in any sport."

Describing a swimmer's ordeal before a race, Spitz recalled the Munich games, where "we waited in a small place about the size of a motel bedroom," he said, "the eight of us in our different sweat-suit gear, the sound of 20,000 people outside beating at the wall, and we would watch the race preceding ours on a monitor. We were really like stage performers. They would knock at the door and call out, 'O.K., you're on.'"

Having topped the previous Olympic records of four gold medals won by Don Schollander in the 1968 swimming events and by Jesse Owens in track and field (1936), Spitz was suddenly tired of swimming. A price was paid, he said, for "all that work. There is something very depressing about being the best in the world at something. I was programmed for all those years. I swam $2\frac{1}{2}$ hours in the morning and 2 in the evening, maybe seven miles a day for six years, and during all those hours I'd think about getting out of the pool at the end of the session and how pleasant that was going to be. I loved to think about getting out. But I became the best in the world."

Spitz in the midst of his gold-medal sweep at the 1972 Olympics, Neil Leifer, Photograph, Sports Illustrated

Union Pond, Williamsburg, L.I., Thomas & Eno after Winslow Homer, Lithograph, c. 1863, Museum of the City of New York

I C E   S K A T I N G

Biographies by
AMY HENDERSON

JACKSON HAINES (1840–1879)

Called "The American Skating King," Jackson Haines virtually invented the art of figure skating. Before the late nineteenth century, ice skating in America consisted mainly of the rather stiff execution of "figures." Haines transformed this robotry into spectacle with his high sense of style: he set skating to music, donned colorful theatrical costumes, and performed balletic routines on the ice. It was his flamboyance which revolutionized figure skating as a sport and gave it, for the first time, a general popularity.

Haines had gone to Europe, when he was ten, to study dance. He returned to America and, at the age of seventeen, became a theatrical apprentice. It was in this period that he began to apply dance movements to skating. He also changed the skate itself—formerly a blade which had to be fastened to the boot—by fusing the two, thereby greatly enhancing the skate's overall stability. Haines then developed some of his most dramatic movements, particularly the "sit-spin," which today is still called the "Jackson Haines."

Haines gave exhibitions at rinks and fairs on the East Coast and in Canada, but failed to win much public enthusiasm for his new style of skating. He went to England during the winter of 1864–65, but again met with little popular success. In fact, Victorian circles were aghast at his "fancy skating." From England Haines went on to tour the capitals of Europe. And here, finally, he earned great acclaim. His appearances in Vienna were nothing short of triumphant, and he soon had the entire city waltzing on ice. Haines founded the Vienna school of skating, which developed into the international style in use today.

Haines was the first ice-skating figure to achieve worldwide celebrity, but when he died, it was in relative obscurity in a small Finnish town. Much of his lasting importance has derived from his extensive teaching, and the subsequent transmission by his students of his particular art. Haines's style of skating—the special movements, figures, and sense of theatricality—permanently transformed the sport.

Jackson Haines, Unidentified artist, Oil on canvas, Date unknown, Dick Button

STAR OF THE ICE... STAR OF THE DANCE... AND A WOMAN AGLOW WITH ROMANCE

INTERNATIONAL PICTURES, INC.

presents

SONJA HENIE

in

"It's A Pleasure!"

IN TECHNICOLOR

with

MICHAEL O'SHEA

MARIE McDONALD

BILL JOHNSON

GUS SCHILLING

Directed by

WM. A. SEITER

Produced by

DAVID LEWIS

SCREEN PLAY BY LYNN STARLING AND ELLIOT PAUL

An International Picture

Released through RKO-RADIO PICTURES, Inc

GOOD ENTERTAINMENT IS "INTERNATIONAL"

180

SONJA HENIE (1912–1969)

When Sonja Henie came to the United States to stage her first ice carnival in 1936, she was embraced by the press as "The Norwegian Doll." Only twenty-four, she had already won ten consecutive world championships and three Olympic gold medals (1928, 1932, and 1936). America went into an ice-skating fervor: thousands attended her shows, little girls begged for "Sonja Henie dolls," and everyone who was brave enough tried to imitate the figures Sonja cut on ice at 40 mph.

The Nordic Golden Girl was a petite 5'2", blond, and engaging. Americans would idolize her in the 1940s as Europeans had since she won the Norwegian National championship at the age of ten. The 75-pound Sonja told her family then, "I want to win the world's championship." When she competed in her first Olympics in 1924, she was only twelve. She performed in short skirts and white skates, and the press called her *"Das Wunderkind."* Though she finished last that year, experts noted that "future aspirants for the world title will have to reckon with Sonja Henie of Norway, already a great performer who has every gift—personality, form, strength, speed and nerve." In 1926 Sonja finished second in the world competition. It was the last time she ever lost.

She won the first of her string of world championships in 1927. She also saw Pavlova dance that year, and afterward called the event the greatest influence in her life. Sonja enthusiastically adopted ballet into her skating routines, pioneering its use on ice and introducing choreographic design into her free skating. In 1928, the sixteen-year-old skater overwhelmed 211 competitors in the Winter Olympics at St. Moritz, and her ballet-like movements set a trend. She won her second gold medal for women's figure skating at Lake Placid in 1932, and her third in Bavaria in 1936.

After the 1936 Olympics, she turned professional and came to the United States, where she was hailed as "The Pavlova of the Silver Blades." In four exhibitions at Madison Square Garden soon after her arrival, Sonja entertained more than ninety thousand people. She also quickly embarked on what was to become a fabulously successful screen career. Darryl F. Zanuck of Twentieth Century-Fox signed her up after watching her skate at a Hollywood exhibition. "I was electrified by her," he said. "There will never be another like her." He offered her a contract for $10,000, but she demanded, and got, one worth ten times that. Her first film, *One in a Million,* was released at the end of 1936 to raves. The New York *Times* critic found the skating queen "like a transfigured Degas ballerina." Her second film, *Thin Ice,* was released in 1937 and touted as "one of the brightest comedies of the year." Her films showed the American public an artistic style of skating which had never before been seen on such a large scale. They were great box-office successes and, in ten years of filming, Sonja became a millionaire several times over.

In 1938, she organized the first of the extravagant ice spectaculars—her Hollywood Ice Revues—which she would take on tour in leading American cities until the early 1950s. Her 1952 revue, notable for its grand costumes and exotic ice-ballet routines, was said by *Variety* to show "Miss Henie's ice virtuosity . . . at its peak."

Sonja Henie made ice skating an important sport in America. Once a rich man's hobby, skating won wide popularity because of her. Artificial rinks sprang up all over the country, and Sonja Henie Junior Olympics Clubs enrolled forty thousand members in the wake of her first national tour in 1936.

After four decades of what has been called one of the most consistently brilliant athletic careers ever, Sonja Henie died of leukemia in 1969, at the age of fifty-seven.

◄ *Sonia Henie became America's sweetheart on skates in a series of Hollywood films in the 1930s and 1940s,* National Portrait Gallery, Smithsonian Institution

Dick Button's acrobatic agility revolutionized men's figure skating,
Dick Button

DICK BUTTON (b. 1929)

The preeminent men's champion of post–World War II figure skating was Dick Button, who pioneered the modern style of free skating. He had started to figure skate at the age of twelve, but without much success. Once, while the 5'2", 160-pound boy stood listening, his instructor told his father that any future lessons would be a waste of money: "Never in a million years could your son become a good figure skater. He lacks coordination." Swiss-born coach Gus Lussi began working with him in 1942, helping Button develop the bold free-skating routines which opened the sport to greater expression. When he was fourteen, the now 5'10", 175-pound youth won the Men's National Novice championship and, two years later, he became the U.S. Men's Figure Skating Champion, the youngest ever to win that title.

At the 1948 Winter Olympics, Dick Button stunned the world by becoming the first person from the United States to win an Olympic gold medal in figure skating. When he entered Harvard that fall, he held every major men's figure-skating title there was, notably the World, European, Olympic, and U.S. championships—an unparalleled accomplishment. In 1949, he became the first winter athlete to be awarded the James E. Sullivan Memorial Trophy as America's outstanding amateur athlete. During the four years Button studied at Harvard, he continued to skate in competition. He was U.S. National Champion from 1946 to 1952, World Champion from 1948 to 1952, and North American Titlist from 1947 to 1952. And, in the 1952 Winter Games, he capped his amateur career by successfully defending his Olympic championship.

Button's incredible technique was an important factor in his accumulation of titles, but his real contribution to the sport lay in the revolutionary innovations he made in freestyle skating. He was the first in competition to execute successfully such movements as the double Axel Paulson jump (named after the pioneer Norwegian speed-skating champion of the 1880s), three consecutive double-loop jumps, the triple-loop jump, and the "Button" (or flying) camel spin. These multiple-rotation jumps and flying spins transformed skating to such an extent that much of the athletic content of competition figure skating today is based on Button's inventions. One feat was especially sensational. Few skaters could execute the "double Axel," which required a performer to skate backward, make a tremendous leap into a two-and-a-half body spin, land with feather lightness, and leave a smooth blade-cut in the ice. But Button, not content with his effortless accomplishment of this routine, invented the "double double Axel," in which he did two of these movements—one right after the other—over thirty feet of ice in about two seconds.

Having conquered every amateur challenge available, he turned professional after his win at the 1952 Olympics. Barely twenty-one, he was just old enough to sign a contract for $150,000 to star in the Ice Capades that year. He then went on to organize and skate in his own ice shows, while at the same time completing his Harvard law degree in 1955. He has written extensively on skating—especially *Dick Button on Skates* (1955) and *Instant Skating* (1964)—and has become increasingly involved in the production of television sports. A recognized authority on figure skating, he is a familiar on-camera commentator for most major televised skating competitions.

The American skating team at the 1948 Winter Olympics, Button at center, Dick Button

Tenley Albright, Hy Peskin, Photograph, 1955, Sports Illustrated

TENLEY ALBRIGHT (b. 1935)

Only two years after she took up figure skating at the age of nine, Tenley Albright was stricken with a mild case of polio—a near-tragedy that, in fact, helped make her a champion. The polio was nonparalytic, though it weakened her abdominal and lower back muscles. Illness gave her the kind of determination and discipline a superior athlete needs, and she was skating again only three months after the attack. Asked if her confidence had ever flagged, she said, "Just once, really—last winter. It was four o'clock in the morning and snowing hard. I was going down the back alley to the skating club with my heavy tape recorder and two pairs of boots and skates in my hands, when suddenly I slipped and everything went flying all around me. I just sat there and said to myself, 'What am I doing here?' I was so alone and there wasn't even anyone to laugh with me." According to her coach, "She'd take a lot of falls, but she'd pick herself up and start all over again." Albright would regularly practice for three or four hours before breakfast and school. As her coach said then, "She's got it in her head and heart and that's why she can make it come out through her feet." In January 1947, four months after her bout with polio, Tenley Albright won the Eastern U.S. Ladies' Junior title.

She competed in her first Olympics at Oslo in 1952, winning an astonishing second place and the silver medal. The next year, at the age of seventeen, she became the first American woman to win the world championship. She also won the U.S. and North American titles that year, thereby becoming this country's first triple-crown figure skater. When she entered Radcliffe in 1953, she continued to compete, winning the U.S. Ladies' Senior Figure Skating title in 1953, 1954, and 1955. Then, in 1956, she became the first American woman to win the Olympic gold medal in figure skating, edging out another young American, fifteen-year-old Carol Heiss, who won the silver medal. When she returned home to Newton, Massachusetts, she was greeted by a crowd of fifty thousand people along a parade route nearly two miles long.

Miss Albright's great strength was her ability to blend aesthetic and athletic skills. To the art of free skating she brought a special grace and fluidity of motion. She contributed several innovations to this aspect of the sport, including a soaring mazurka jump with which she was particularly identified. Although she always scored well on her "school figures"—the sixty-two patterns in which a skater traces and retraces two- and three-lobed figure eights—she particularly enjoyed free skating. "Skating is expression," she has said, adding that it was the creative side which she relished—"the opportunity to practice new jumps or dance steps, to fit them to music in my own way, and then perfect the whole thing."

Her last competition was in 1956, when she defeated rival—and heir—Carol Heiss in the U.S. championships. The contest has been described as a "dazzling" exhibition of skating. Miss Albright won, 1,712.02 total points to 1,691.67 for Miss Heiss.

Following that event, Tenley Albright gave up competitive skating and earned an M.D. at Harvard Medical School. A highly regarded specialist, she is a member of the Sports Medicine Committee of the U.S. Olympics Committee.

PEGGY FLEMING (b. 1948)

In 1961, an airplane crash took the lives of the entire United States figure skating team. Peggy Fleming was only thirteen then, and her coach was among those killed. "For a long time," she said later, "I didn't feel like going out there to skate." But she did, and in 1964, before she was sixteen, she won her first national championship, becoming the youngest U.S. Senior Ladies' Figure Skating champion in history. She also finished sixth in the Winter Olympics that year.

Her confidence boosted, Peggy Fleming focused her determination on winning the 1966 world championship in Davos, Switzerland. Five-foot-three and 109 pounds, she was dubbed "The Bambi of the Blades" by the European press. She trained hard to increase her stamina —her family even moved to Colorado Springs so that she could train in an atmosphere comparable to Davos's mountain air. Her coach, Carlo Fassi, developed a stiff regimen for her, working particularly hard on the "school figures"—the tracing and retracing of two- and three-lobed figure eights—which would account for 60 percent of the total score in competition. "Peggy looks fragile," Coach Fassi noted, "but believe me, she's not." Crowds used to unhinge her, but she overcame this phobia by pretending that the people in the stand were cabbages—"How can you be intimidated by rows of cabbages?"

She won the 1966 world championship, and thereafter never lost a competition. She successfully defended her world crown in 1967 and 1968, and the U.S. National championship title five times from 1964 to 1968. The culmination of her competitive career came at the 1968 Grenoble Olympics, where she resoundingly won the gold medal for women's figure skating. The New York *Times* called it "a victory of the ballet over the Ice Follies approach to figure skating."

Peggy Fleming was very strong in her execution of compulsory figures, but she also skated with a balletic grace. She had a steel-like strength, which allowed her to perform such difficult skating movements as the "spread-eagle double Axel spread-eagle"—a combination of acrobatic movements (leaping in the air from a backward-leaning spread-eagle position, spinning two and a half times in mid-air, and landing back in the same position) which no other woman in international competition has ever been able to master. Dick Button has said that she was "a unique combination of athletic ability, technical control, great style, and immense musicality." She was delicate in performance rather than fiery. "With some skaters," Button went on, "there is a lot of fuss and feathers, but nothing is happening. With Peggy, there's no fuss and feathers, and a great deal is happening."

Since retiring from competition in 1968, Miss Fleming has become a well-known television personality and a featured performer for the Ice Follies and Holiday on Ice, where she has continued to win over audiences withher ballerina quality and sense of drama.

Peggy Fleming, John Z. Zimmerman, ▶
Photograph, 1968, Sports Illustrated

ERIC HEIDEN (b. 1958)

Eric Heiden's performance at the 1980 Winter Olympics, during which he won gold medals in each of the five men's speed-skating events, established him as the best men's speed skater in history. At the previous Olympics, seventeen-year-old Eric had finished an unobtrusive nineteenth in the 5,000-meter and seventh in the 1,500-, but the next year (1977) he traveled to the Dutch city of Heerenveen and, with remarkable efforts in four grueling races ranging from the 500-meter sprint to the 10,000-meter marathon, broke from obscurity to become the men's speed-skating champion of the world. He continued to build his confidence by sweeping the field in European races during the next two years, and repeated as world champion in Sweden in 1978 and Norway in 1979. The Norwegians, for whom speed skating is as much a part of the national marrow as baseball and football are for America, adopted the boyish Heiden as a folk hero. His profile appeared on milk cartons as well as sports pages, and songs and books were written about him. In Oslo and Amsterdam, he commanded more adoration than rock singers.

But it was not until the "Great Whoopee"—Eric's term for the hoopla surrounding the 1980 Olympics at Lake Placid—that an epidemic of Heiden fever boiled America's blood. Eric Heiden went for the gold with electrifying derring-do, hurtling his body around the ice oval with such speed that he consistently covered the distance of five football fields in between thirty and forty seconds. Although he is 6'1", Eric's 185 pounds seemed concentrated in his twenty-nine-inch thighs, which moved like pistons as he pumped out meter after meter on the ice.

At Lake Placid, he captured four Olympic gold medals—in the 500-meter, 1,000-meter, 1,500-meter, and 5,000-meter events—before taking a break to scream his lungs out at the U.S.–Soviet hockey game. "He left there thinking he could conquer the world," his coach said. In the 10,000-meter finale the next day, he won his fifth gold—an Olympic record—by an astonishing margin of 7.9 seconds over his nearest competitor. Later, when asked what he would do with all his medals, Eric guessed that "they'll probably sit in my mom's dresser where the rest of them are." He never really skated for the glory of it all so much as for the pure joy. "American skaters have no other reason to skate except for the fun of it," he explained just before the start of the games. "We're out to have a good time, and I think that's why we win."

As for the future, Eric Heiden hopes to slip back into relative obscurity, do some bicycle racing perhaps, and study sports medicine. "I don't want people to put me on a pedestal," he worries. "I want to stay just the way I am now. I'd really be uptight if people were always praising me and stuff like that." But he also knows that life will never be the same. "I guess it's something I'm going to have to get used to."

◀ *Speed skater Eric Heiden,* Heinz Kleutmeier,
Photograph, 1980, Sports Illustrated

Hurdlers at the U.S. Olympic Trials at Palo Alto, George Silk, Photograph, 1959, TIME Inc.

TRACK

Biographies by
MARC PACHTER

THE ILLUSTRATED SPORTING & DRAMATIC NEWS

REGISTERED AT THE GENERAL POST-OFFICE FOR TRANSMISSION ABROAD.

No. 105.—VOL. IV. SATURDAY, FEBRUARY 19, 1876. PRICE SIXPENCE
By Post 6½D.

EDWARD PAYSON WESTON, THE FAMOUS AMERICAN PEDESTRIAN.

Edward Payson Weston, champion walker of the nineteenth century, Library of Congress

EDWARD PAYSON WESTON (1839–1929)

Edward Payson Weston began his career as a long-distance walker quite by accident. Having lost a bet that the next President of the United States would not be Abraham Lincoln, he paid the penalty: a walk from Boston to Washington in ten consecutive days to see Lincoln inaugurated on the afternoon of March 4, 1861. As word of the wager spread, Weston became a celebrity, cheered on from town to town and fed with sandwiches and doughnuts as he kept his stride. Pausing only to catnap, he arrived at 5:00 p.m., too late to see Lincoln sworn in but in time to dance at his inaugural ball. The prize was a bag of peanuts.

Six years later, the stakes had gone up considerably. For a bet of $10,000, Weston was challenged to walk the 1,237 miles from Portland, Maine, to Chicago, Illinois, in twenty-six days out of thirty (excluding Sundays). Accompanied by six men in a carriage to keep him honest, the elegant Weston, dressed in his walking-costume of short jacket, tight breeches, silk derby, and gloves, maintained his sprightly, effortless pace at a speed of 3 to 5 mph. Not the first of the professional walkers, or even the fastest, he kept the crowds which lined the route fascinated by his nonchalance and endurance. When he reached Chicago in the allotted time, newspapers everywhere hailed the "Great Pedestrian Feat," and bettors collected their winnings.

A sports hero for a genteel age, Weston preached the moral and physical virtues of long-distance walking. But, for all his piety, he was a committed athlete and a marvelous showman. In 1871, on an indoor track, he did 112 miles in twenty-four hours, to the cheers of paying customers. Three years later, after considerable frustration, he finally attained his goal of 500 miles in six days, again on what he called the "circular monotonous round."

By 1876, he felt himself ready to take on the Jerusalem of walkers—England. The English hooted the presumptuous Yankee until he proved, by walking 1,015 miles during his first five weeks, that he was worthy of their hiking traditions. Three years later, he flabbergasted his hosts by winning the Astley Belt, signifying world supremacy in walking, for covering 550 miles of indoor track in 142 hours. The favorite, "Blower" Brown, was left huffing 100 miles behind. So popular did Weston become in England that he was invited back four years later for a stunt meant to publicize the temperance movement. "Payse" walked 50 miles a day for a hundred days, from November 1883 to March 1884, delivering sermons on the evils of drink.

For decades Weston's walking, sponsored by sporting men and corporations, was the talk of America. Bulletins were posted on his progress; fan programs sold along the way lovingly recorded his past achievements. Every now and then, as he grew older, a committee of examining physicians would astonish the press with an announcement that the champion's body was ageless. To prove it, at age sixty-eight he repeated his celebrated Portland–Chicago walk. Covering a route nineteen miles longer, he bettered his record of forty years before by twenty-nine hours. At seventy he walked 3,895 miles from New York to San Francisco, switching his legs with a rod he carried to encourage them on. The effort must count among the most heroic of physical achievements. Facing extremes of heat and cold, he was forced at one point to crawl for miles on his hands and knees against the powerful winds. But he made it—in 104 days and 7 hours—and returned the following year in less than 77 days. He slowed down to the pace of lesser mortals only in his late eighties, and died at ninety, forgotten with the sport he had honored.

JIM THORPE (1887–1953)

In the official records of the 1912 Olympics held at Stockholm, there is no mention at all of the American Indian Jim Thorpe. Victory at the pentathlon, a grueling five-event contest including the running broad jump, the javelin throw, the 200-meter flat race, the discus throw, and the 1,500-meter race, is accorded to one F. R. Bie of Norway. The gold-medal winner of the decathlon, whose ten events comprise the 100-meter dash, running broad jump, shot put, running high jump, 400-meter flat race, discus throw, 110-meter high hurdles, pole vault, javelin throw, and 1,500-meter race, is listed as Hugo Wieslander of Sweden. But the records belie the reality. It was Jim Thorpe who was given a hero's tribute by an enraptured sporting world; Thorpe who was hailed by King Gustave of Sweden as "the greatest athlete in the world." When he answered, "Thanks, King," Bie and Wieslander were footnotes to the most memorable Olympic performance of all time. In the pentathlon Thorpe's score was more than twice as good as Bie's. In the decathlon he logged 8,412.96 points to Wieslander's 7,724. Laden with two gold medals, a bronze bust of the King, and a great silver chalice in the shape of a Viking ship, awarded by Gustave in special tribute, Thorpe stood at the pinnacle of athletic honor.

Within a year he had toppled from Mt. Olympus. Because Thorpe had played some seasons of semiprofessional baseball during a break in his studies at Carlisle, a government-sponsored school for Indians in Pennsylvania, regulation-quoting Amateur Athletic Union officials had his name expunged from the Olympic record books in 1913, unmoved by his plea of innocent motive. Other baseball players on leave from college had taken the precaution of assuming false names to retain their amateur status; and Thorpe had not realized that his was in jeopardy. "I did not play for the money there was in it," he explained, "but because I liked to play ball."

Indeed he did. With little practice and less premeditation, the most extraordinary athlete of our time competed in every imaginable sport just for the joy of it. Track had been only one of his specialties at Carlisle. His coach, "Pop" Warner, who had sent him to Stockholm after watching him develop into the school's virtual one-man track and field team, saw in him as well the makings of a great football player. In the crucial game of the 1911 season, Thorpe scored four field goals and ran seventy yards for a touchdown and victory against Harvard, whose philosophical coach, Percy Haughton, pronounced him the "super-player" everyone dreamed of. The next season, after his Olympic competition, Thorpe scored twenty-five touchdowns and 198 points. In the legendary Army game that year, he ran ninety-five yards after kickoff straight to the end zone. Literally, there was no stopping him.

Legend has made of Thorpe a tragic figure, blighted by his Olympic heartbreak; but in fact, after the shock passed, he went on to flourish in professional sports. He played major-

◄ *Before his senior year at Carlisle University, Jim Thorpe astonished the world with his pentathlon and decathlon victories at the 1912 Olympics in Stockholm,* United Press International

Thorpe in a javelin throw, Culver Pictures

league baseball for six solid, if not spectacular, years, and then began in 1915, after the baseball season was over, the first of nearly twenty years of professional football. He made the Canton Bulldogs a power to be reckoned with, and from that Ohio bastion bolstered the appeal of the professional game. A star attraction whenever he played, the great Thorpe offered to pay a thousand dollars to any team that could prevent him from going ten yards in four downs. He kept his money. In 1920, when the American Professional Football Association, later the National Football League, was formed, Thorpe was named its first president.

It was only after his body began to go that pathos overwhelmed his life. The sad obscurity of Thorpe's later years was relieved occasionally when a reporter decided to do an update; or when Hollywood made use of him, for one shining moment, as the subject of *Jim Thorpe, All-American*, starring Burt Lancaster; or during periodic fruitless attempts to reinstate his Olympic records. He died in poverty in 1953, three years after a poll of sportswriters proclaimed him—and not Ruth or Dempsey or Cobb—the outstanding athlete of the century.

Thorpe seen drop-kicking late in his professional career, Bettmann Archive, Inc.

While at Carlisle, Thorpe played spectacular college football; he later went on to a professional career, Culver Pictures

Babe Didrikson in a broad jump, 1931, United Press International

BABE DIDRIKSON (1914–1956)

The few reporters assigned to cover women athletes, in the dark ages of the 1930s, first noticed the exploits of a young Texas clerical worker on the basketball courts of amateur competition. Babe Didrikson, star of the Employers Casualty Company of Dallas, led her company team, the Golden Cyclones, to an Amateur Athletic Union national championship and two runner-up spots, from 1930 to 1932, scoring an incredible 106 points in one game. She stirred the sports backwater even more when she entered track and field competition. At the Olympic tryouts of 1932, her performance was one for the books. In the eight events she entered, Babe won six gold medals and broke four world records. She astonished the crowds by taking the team title single-handedly with thirty points. Second place went to the twenty-two members of the Illinois Women's Athletic Club, who together scored twenty-two points. "Miss Mildred Didrikson of Dallas, Texas, who prefers to be called 'Babe,' " wrote an admiring reporter, "will lead the American women's Olympic track and field team. Such assistance as she may need against the foreign invasion will be provided by fifteen other young ladies."

Didrikson's teammates were less than pleased by this kind of publicity and the arrogance it bred in her. But the Babe's swagger became good copy at the Los Angeles Olympics. "I came out here to beat everybody in sight," she boasted, "and that's just what I'm going to do. Sure I can do anything." Her grandstanding drew the limelight to women's track and field and made a national star of her when she took the gold in the javelin throw (her first try broke the world record by more than 11 feet) and the 80-meter hurdles. "Whatta-gal!" erupted the headline writers. Grantland Rice, dean of sportswriters, added his benediction: "She is beyond all belief until you see her perform. Then you finally understand that you are looking at the most flawless section of muscle harmony, of complete mental and physical coordination the world of sport has ever seen."

Had Didrikson been less of a showwoman, she would have faded from sight after her glory year, but she was too determined and too talented to let that happen. Billed as the athlete who could do anything, she went barnstorming throughout America for years—as a vaudeville performer running on a treadmill, as star pitcher for the otherwise bearded House of David exhibition baseball team, as captain and often lone woman on the Babe Didrikson

Didrikson, shown here at the 1932 Olympics in Los Angeles, was the leading women's track and field star of her day, Wide World Photos, Inc.

Didrikson in 1931, United Press International

Didrikson's greatest successes came on the amateur and professional golf circuits, Wide World Photos, Inc.

All-American Basketball Team. In exhibition matches, she pitched for the Dodgers against the Phillies, and the Cardinals against the Athletics, and even managed to strike out Joe DiMaggio. She worked out with the Southern Methodist University football team, made a cross-country billiards tour, and another tour with golfer Gene Sarazen.

It was a way to make money, but not sports history, and Didrikson wanted that chance again. Reinstated as an amateur in 1944, she brought her flair and ferocious competitive edge to women's golf. The crown jewel of her amateur years, victory sixteen in a string of seventeen winning tournaments, was her triumph at the British "Ladies Amateur" tourney in Scotland, the first by an American. Babe, now married to George Zaharias, was greeted, when she returned on the *Queen Mary*, by a tugboat rented by her husband loaded with more than seventy writers and photographers. On her return to their home in Denver, she was cheered by a crowd estimated at fifty thousand.

An institution now, Didrikson gave up her amateur status and formed, with Patty Berg, the Ladies Professional Golf Association. In her first year as a pro, the nine tournaments on the Women's Tour offered a combined, meager total of $15,000, but Didrikson's flair and Berg's energy would bring new interest to the game. The Babe's 250-yard drives, her ability to joke with the galleries and to give the press something to write about, paid off for all woman professionals. By the early 1950s, testimonials to her determination and spirit took on new meaning when she had an operation for cancer and then returned to win the 1954 U.S. Women's Open championship, an unheard-of twelve strokes ahead of her nearest competitor. Didrikson won five events in all that year and received, for the sixth time, the Associated Press Woman Athlete of the Year award. Her vigorous life was ended by cancer two years

later.

JESSE OWENS (1913–1980)

More than a year before Jesse Owens earned international fame as the hero of the Berlin Olympics, he had the single most perfect day in the history of modern track competition. A sophomore representing Ohio State in the Big Ten championships at Ann Arbor, Michigan, Owens dashed, broad jumped, and hurdled his way to three world records and a tie, all in less than an hour. The succession of triumphs began with a 9.4-second 100-yard dash, matching the world record; this was followed ten minutes later by a broad jump of 26'8¾", more than half a foot better than the previous record, and good enough to stand for twenty years; by the 200-yard dash, at an unprecedented 20.3 seconds; and by the 220-yard low hurdles at a record-breaking 22.6 seconds. It was an incredible exhibition not only of speed and grace but of determination. Owens had sprained his back weeks before the meet and had been advised to withdraw for fear of permanent damage. Unable even to jog at the pre-meet warm-up, he decided nevertheless to compete: "My back hurt when I went into the starting crouch," he remembered. "But when the starter said 'Get set,' I felt no pain at all."

Owens was a phenomenon but not yet a legend. That developed during six days the following year, when, in the course of an Olympics constructed by Nazi Germany to glorify the Aryan ideal, he competed in twelve preliminary heats and official events and managed to break or equal Olympic records nine times. One hundred sixty-three pounds when he started

Jesse Owens on the track,
National Archives

201

the competition, Owens wound up twenty-four pounds lighter and four gold medals heavier, winning the 100-meter and 200-meter sprints, the broad jump, and, with his teammates, the 400-meter relay.

Too much has been made of Hitler's alleged refusal to shake Owens's hand. The German leader had stopped congratulating victors publicly two days before the black champion began competing—perhaps because he anticipated embarrassment. Owens was not singled out for a snub and, in any case, gave little thought to Hitler and his rituals. Owens's glorification, in the newspapers of America, as "deadly poison to Nordic Supremacy," in the words of Grantland Rice, meant less to him than his conquest of the German spectators at Berlin who cherished him as a supreme athlete. In Leni Riefenstahl's glorious documentary *Olympia*, commissioned by the German authorities for their own purposes, it is Owens who hypnotizes the cameras and leaves a lasting impression of physical grace beyond all propaganda.

After the limelight faded, the champion faced an uncertain future as a retired competitor. For a while he had his own basketball team, the Jesse Owens Olympians. In time he was reduced to traveling from town to town to challenge all comers to race him, giving himself a ten-yard disadvantage. His most celebrated stunt was a race against a horse in Havana. "People said it was degrading for an Olympic champion to run against a horse," Owens later said, "but what was I supposed to do? I had four gold medals but you can't eat four gold medals. There was no television, no big advertising, no endorsements then. You know, I didn't even get the Sullivan Award. Never. In 1935, the year I broke three world records and tied one in one day it went to some golfer named Lawson Little. And in 1936 the AAU gave it to Glenn Morris, who won the decathlon in Berlin. A lot of people don't realize what blacks had to do then to earn money."

The story has a happy ending. Owen's optimism and energy survived the bad years and became the basis for a career in public relations. Voted by sportswriters in 1950 the finest track star of the half-century, he returned to Berlin the following year, his first visit since the Olympics. During a track meet, the champion, in his old Olympic suit, jogged around the stadium as seventy-five thousand Germans cheered. The magic had never died.

With no professional track circuit available to him, Owens was reduced to exhibition matches in the years follow-ing his Olympic victory. Here he is at California's Bay Meadows Race Track in 1948, Wide World Photos, Inc.

Owens, victorious at the 1936 Berlin Olympics, won the affection of the German crowds despite Nazi propaganda, Wide World Photos, Inc.

Jesse Owens, Joseph Brown, Bronze, 1942, Collection of the artist

*Only months after his high school coach introduced the seventeen-year-old Bob Mathias
to the decathlon, he won the gold medal in the 1948 London Olympics,* Robert Mathias

BOB MATHIAS (b. 1930)

By all logic, Bob Mathias should never have been ready to compete in the 1948 London Olympics. Four months before, the young Tulare, California, track star had never even heard of the decathlon. In the course of breaking more than twenty high-school records, he had shown talent in the shot put, the discus throw, the high hurdles, and the high jump, but not enough to qualify for Olympic competition. His coach, Virgil Jackson, hit upon the perfect test of his versatility. "He came to me," Mathias later recalled, "and suggested I try the decathlon. I asked him what a decathlon was. He said it was ten events, but he didn't know which ones. I said if he could find out, I could try 'em." Of the ten events, he had no experience at all with the javelin throw or the pole vault. Yet, less than a month later, he took his first championship at the Pacific Coast Games in Pasadena, California. Two weeks after that, he defeated the three-time national champion, Irving "Moon" Mondschein, at the Amateur Athletic Union Olympic tryouts and became, overnight, America's prime contender. The only one not surprised was seventeen-year-old Mathias.

As the youngest American ever fielded for an Olympic track team, Mathias was a celebrity even before competition began. He never seemed to think that he was at a disadvantage against more than thirty other more experienced entrants in the international decathlon. By the end of the rainy first day, five events down, he was a respectable third. The next day, colder and wetter than the first, Mathias made his bid. Despite a bad start in the hurdles, and a stroke of bad luck when he was assigned a lesser score after the mud had obscured the place where his discus landed, he was ahead by the third event of the day, the pole vault. The next-to-last event began at 10:00 p.m. in the poorly lit gloom of the London stadium. With his second try, Mathias made a winning javelin throw of 165'1". The last event, the 1,500-meter, brought him safely to victory with forty-nine seconds to spare, and an overall total of 7,139 points. He had exceeded Jim Thorpe's 1912 unofficial record in all but the 100-meter dash and the 1,500-meter run. "In rain, on a track covered with water . . . in fading light, and finally under floodlights, it was an amazing achievement," wrote Allison Danzig of the New York *Times*.

Bob was certain that he would never do it again, but four years later, in 1952, while a student at Stanford University, he was back in Olympics competition for another round of physical punishment. This time he was the clear favorite. In the intervening years, he had won the National Decathlon championship three more times and was now a ripe twenty-one years of age. By the end of the first day in Helsinki, it was already clear that Mathias was going to take the gold. The youngest decathlon winner in Olympic history became the Olympics' only two-time decathlon winner as well. His point total, 7,887, broke his own world record, and he bettered every 1948 event—including the javelin throw, with a score of just over 194 feet. Politics made the victory even sweeter. At the height of the cold war, the Russians had fielded their first Olympic team since 1908. "There were many more pressures on American athletes because of the Russians than in 1948," Mathias later said. "They were in a sense the real enemy. You just had to beat 'em." When he returned home, there were very few Americans left who had never heard of the decathlon.

WILMA RUDOLPH (b. 1940)

Wilma Rudolph had to relearn to walk before she could run. After an early childhood bout of double pneumonia and scarlet fever had left her left leg paralyzed, she went through years of confinement to bed or chair before she was back on her feet at age eight, with the use of special shoes. It did not take long for her body to find its natural tone. By thirteen, she had made her high-school basketball team and, at fifteen, was a certified athletic marvel, known throughout the black community of Clarksville, Tennessee, as an all-state player who had scored 803 points in twenty-five games. Her coach, Clinton Gray, who called her "Skeeter" (for mosquito) because she was "always buzzing around," took up the suggestion of the great track coach Ed Temple to start her running. After one year she had already qualified, at sixteen, for a place on the 1956 Olympic team at Melbourne, where she shared in a bronze-medal win for the 400-meter relay.

But that was all prelude. Within one year she was running full time for Ed Temple at Tennessee Agricultural and Industrial State College in the best women's track program in the nation. Rudolph's genius was honed by hard competition. "Her teammates are the next three fastest girls in the country," said her coach. "Rudolph runs fast because she is pressed so hard in practice. Without it she wouldn't be nearly as good as she is." Temple's point was proven when the entire 400-meter women's relay team for the 1960 Olympics was chosen out of his squad.

Never able to count on her health, Rudolph went through a debilitating illness which canceled her 1958 track season, a pulled left thigh muscle in 1959, and serious complications from a tonsil operation in the Olympic year of 1960. But, when it was time to go to Rome, she was ready. How ready became obvious in her first event, the 100-meter dash, when she broke away from the competition at the halfway point and won, three yards ahead of the silver medalist, in 11 seconds flat. Her second Olympic record and gold medal came in the 200-meter dash, at 24 seconds, when she again showed the stride which, one reporter wrote, "made the rest of the pack seem to be churning on a treadmill." The Rudolph trademark was composure—a quality of smooth, effortless, impassive speed. Her third gold medal came to her, as if by right, when she anchored the United States 400-meter relay team: Wilma and her Tennessee A & I classmates set both world and Olympic marks at 44.5 seconds.

On tour throughout Europe with her teammates, Rudolph was hailed as a goddess of sport. "*La Gazella Nera*" (Black Gazelle) to the Italians, "*La Perle Noire*" (Black Pearl) and "*La Chattanooga Choo Choo*" to the French, she was mobbed wherever she went. Once her shoes were pulled off her feet. A wax statue was made of her in Madame Tussaud's London Museum. Overwhelmed by the hoopla, she returned to America for a new round of celebrations, banquets, and carnivals in her honor. Winning gold medals must have seemed easier.

She had not finished yet. Runner-up in 1960 for the Amateur Athletic Union's Sullivan trophy as outstanding amateur of the year, she took it that next year, only the third woman to do so. She was the first woman in thirty years to be invited to participate in the celebrated Millrose Games at Madison Square Garden, where she was clocked at 6.9 seconds in the 60-yard dash, tying her own world record. She trimmed it to 6.8 seconds at the New York Athletic Club games two weeks later. By the end of the year, she owned the world's records for the 70-yard dash and the 100-meter event. That was enough. She retired, at the height of her glory, to the quieter life of a schoolteacher.

◀ *Wilma Rudolph hitting the tape in her gold-medal-winning 400-meter relay race at the 1960 Rome Olympics,* Wide World Photos, Inc.

JIM RYUN (b. 1947)

The first time the sporting world noticed the young miler Jim Ryun, of Wichita, Kansas, was in 1964, when he came in last in a field of eight. At seventeen, Ryun, running in his first major race against the toughest competition going, was clocked in at 3 minutes 59 seconds—and became the youngest athlete to break the 4-minute mile. In the Olympic trials that summer, the lanky runner kept everyone interested in him when he spurted from seventh to third place in the 1,500-meter and earned a spot on the United States team. Inexperienced and down with a cold, he only got as far as the semifinals at Tokyo.

So far Ryun was all potential. But then came the first of his three glory years. In 1965, while a freshman at Kansas University, he beat the world record holder, New Zealander Peter Snell, in 3 minutes 55.3 seconds, an American record. The next year Ryun, who had set his sights on Michel Jazy's new mark of 3 minutes 53.6 seconds, broke through to his own world mark of 3 minutes 51.3 seconds. He also set a world record in the half-mile. When he exceeded his own mark, in 1967, with a heroic 3 minutes 51.1 seconds, the world was his. That record would stand as his monument for nine years.

Then things began to go wrong. Shy and introspective, Ryun brooded about the fragility of his fame. The pleasure he took in the personal challenge of running became strained by pressures to stay on top and by his doubts about the loyalty of the crowds. "It was like going into the arena," he once said of his championship meets. "If you don't win, the lions will eat you up." So far, he was a winner, but his worries increased with the onrush of a series of injuries and ailments in 1967 and 1968, the most troubling of them a severe case of mononucleosis in the spring before the Summer Olympics at Mexico City. Favored to bring America its first gold medal, in the 1,500-meter race, in more than sixty years, Ryun was undone by the city's altitude of 7,350 feet and the brilliant performance of Kenya's Kipchoge Keino, who outpaced him throughout the race. The silver medalist suffered two more defeats the following summer at the National Collegiate Athletic Association and the Amateur Athletic Union championships. In the second meet, he gave up midway in the mile, and retired from competition and the harsh glare of publicity. The lions had pounced.

Nineteen months later, in 1971, he was back. With the crowds pulling for him, Ryun took on the brash Marty Liquori, victor of the 1969 NCAA and AAU meets, in the Martin Luther King Freedom Games in Philadelphia. Theirs was the glamour event of the day, a duel touted by the publicists as the "Dream Mile." The soft-spoken Ryun, whose record was six seconds better than Liquori's at his fastest, was the favorite. But his legendary finishing kick failed him. "I'd heard," Liquori said afterward, "if you didn't kill him off early he'd kill you at the finish. All the last lap I kept waiting for him to pass me." To fend off Ryun, Liquori had to run faster than he had ever run, but he won—by five feet.

After that, Ryun ran a number of good races, but attention seemed to focus on the heartbreaking ones. He was called erratic and star-crossed. But he remained a popular figure, with most fans behind him. They shared his final disappointment, which came at the 1972 Munich Olympics. Running in the third lap of the 1,500-meter heat race to qualify for the medal competition, Ryun, who needed only to come in fifth, tripped over the foot of a Ghanaian runner and came in ninth. Then America's greatest miler, who would soon give up amateur competition, walked off the field, comforted by his old rival, Kip Keino.

Jim Ryun setting a new world record for the mile, Rich Clarkson, Photograph, 1966, Sports Illustrated

Polo at Lakewood, George Bellows, Oil on canvas, 1910, Columbus Museum of Art, Ohio

POLO

Biography by
MARC PACHTER

Tommy Hitchcock in 1924,
United Press International

TOMMY HITCHCOCK (1900–1944)

For nearly two decades, between the World Wars, Tommy Hitchcock, Jr., owned polo, and made a gift of it to the thousands of new fans drawn by his exhilarating style of play. Bred to the game by class and family traditions as the son of an early American champion, Hitchcock broke out of the small circle of aristocratic enthusiasts to dominate the headlines of the Golden Age of Sport along with Jack Dempsey, Babe Ruth, Bill Tilden, and Bobby Jones. "We are really an unsnobbish people," observed Paul Gallico. "We don't hold it against a guy for being rich if he can play his game like a true champion and produce those thrills."

Polo began as an American game in 1876, when James Gordon Bennett, publisher of the New York *Herald*, brought it to this country from England. After the formation of the Westchester and Meadow Brook clubs, both of New York, the quality of American play reached the point, in 1886, of international challenge. Great Britain won the first Westchester Cup and kept it until 1909, when the American style of fast-paced action conquered the Cup and revolutionized the game. Though Great Britain won the Cup again in 1914, it was to be their last hurrah. Largely because of Tommy Hitchcock, the British would never again take the championship in the remaining Westchester matches, ending in 1939.

Tommy was the supreme player in the American style. Able above all men to swat a small ball from a speeding horse, he was an aggressive, optimistic scrapper who aimed his mallet for the long hit. When he connected hard, the crowds, reaching up to forty thousand in key matches, would jump to their feet with a roar worthy of football. Bearing down on the ball at a thundering pace, Hitchcock could send it home to a distant goal more than a hundred yards away. No prima donna, he was also a master of passes and intricate maneuver with his three galloping teammates.

Polo has never seen his like. On a scale from 0 to 10, established by the Polo Association to rate players—taking account of horsemanship, hitting ability, "game sense," quality of horses ridden, and sportsmanship—Hitchcock was awarded the highest, 10-goal rating in 1922 and kept it, incredibly, with only one lapse until his retirement in 1939. During his last international appearance, at the three-match Westchester Cup Competition, the thirty-nine-year-old captain scored four of the eleven American winning goals in the first encounter, and four again in the victorious second game which decided the Cup.

His adoring press, excited by "Ten-Goal Tommy's" international victories, including two for the Copa de las Américas (Cup of the Americas) against the third polo power, Argentina, found him good copy in other respects as well. In 1930, his decision to add two Texas cowboys to the American team for the Westchester competition, supposedly scandalizing the snobbish polo world, brought widespread approval. But a more fundamental part of his legend had nothing to do with polo at all. As a seventeen-year-old, too young to qualify for the American Army, Hitchcock had joined France's flying Lafayette Escadrille and shown his fighting spirit, when he was shot down, by escaping wounded from a moving train to rejoin his company. The sportswriters had occasion to remember that during World War II, when Hitchcock, determined to fly again, died in a training accident over England. Tommy Hitchcock was an authentic American hero, twice over.

Gray Matter:
Hitchcock and his opponent deadlocked on the ball, Paul Brown, Pencil, c. 1935, Palm Beach Polo and Country Club, Florida, Paul Brown Collection

Dave Cowens and Nate Thurmond at the opening of the Boston Celtics/Chicago Bulls game, March 1975, Neil Leifer for Sports Illustrated, Photograph, Collection of the photographer

BASKETBALL

Biography by
AMY HENDERSON

Hank Luisetti led Stanford University to basketball preeminence, 1936, Wide World Photos, Inc.

Luisetti goes up for a jump ball in a game between Stanford and Temple, United Press International

HANK LUISETTI (b. 1916)

Born in the same San Francisco neighborhood as Joe DiMaggio, Angelo "Hank" Luisetti began shooting baskets when he was six. By the time he was in high school, he had developed the blistering one-handed shooting style which would revolutionize basketball.

Luisetti perfected his eccentric one-hander at Stanford. In an era when basketball was a deliberately paced sport characterized by two-handed shooting and conventional run-and-jump lay-ups, the slim, 6′3″ forward used his dazzling marksmanship and run-and-shoot style to break the game wide open. Nowhere was this clearer than in a contest held in late 1936 between Stanford and one of the best teams in the East, Long Island University's. Before a crowd of 17,623, packed into Madison Square Garden, Luisetti's ball handling stupefied the LIU team and electrified the sports world as Stanford romped to a 45–31 victory. It was the first time the Easterners had been beaten in three years, and Luisetti received a standing ovation from the New York crowd when he left the court. All-American Art Hillhouse had been assigned to guard him, and Luisetti later said, "I'll never forget the look on Hillhouse's face when I took that first shot. He was about 6′8″ and he never expected a shot like that to be thrown. . . . When it hit I could just see him saying, 'Boy, is this guy lucky.' "

But luck had little to do with it, and never again would basketball be a plodding game of lay-ups and hook shots. Luisetti's one-handed shooting captivated the press. "Some of his shots would have been deemed foolhardy if attempted by anybody else," wrote one reporter, "but with Luisetti's shooting, these were accepted by the enchanted crowd." Luisetti said that "getting all that publicity in New York changed my life. It made me a national figure. . . . I had just been a local kid up to then." It also transformed the sport itself. "I guess we didn't really know what we were starting that night," Luisetti later said. Before long, everyone was imitating that one-hander. "Maybe we didn't realize it at the time, but I think we did bring in the fast break."

By the end of the 1936–37 season, Luisetti had led Stanford to a 25–2 record. Fans clamored to see him flip off his spectacular shots. In Philadelphia, eleven thousand spectators packed an arena to see him play, and in Cleveland he was mobbed by an enthusiastic throng that tried to take his jacket as a souvenir. In his three years of play at Stanford, Luisetti scored a then-record 1,596 points, an average of 16.5 per game, and was three times an All-American. To his coach, he was a "dream player." Luisetti himself stressed his total game rather than any "trick" shooting. "I had flash, but I had more," he has said. "I was all-around. I could shoot long, shoot short, drive, tip rebounds, play defense, and in tough games I was a clutch player. That's when I rose. I laughed a lot, we all did, but inside I guess I had the killer instinct."

After Stanford, Luisetti played in the Amateur Athletic Union and was the game's biggest draw. His presence was said to guarantee an extra $5,000 at the box office. During World War II, he was in the Navy and played service basketball—averaging 30 points a game, a then-amazing figure—until being felled by spinal meningitis in 1944. Though he recovered, he never regained enough strength to play ball again.

GEORGE MIKAN (b. 1924)

When "Big George" Mikan first hurled his 6′10″ and 245 pounds into professional basketball in 1946, he transformed the courts from an arena dominated by quick, small players into a playground for giants. He was the stellar attraction of the National Basketball Association during its formative years (1947–54), when professional basketball was attempting to establish itself as a credible popular sport. Mikan led the Minneapolis Lakers to seven world titles in his eight seasons with them. He made the pro All-Star team six years in a row, and scored 11,376 points in his career—5,000 more than any other player of the period. At a time when college basketball was wracked by scandal, fans flocked to professional games to see this giant break all scoring records.

Mikan had been six feet tall when he was only eleven, and later said that he had been so bitterly self-conscious as a youth "that my height nearly wrecked my life." He played some neighborhood basketball in Joliet, Illinois—with his grandmother often serving as referee—but was too ungainly even to make his high-school team. Yet the coach of DePaul University took a personal interest in Mikan, offering him an athletic scholarship and then putting him on a rigorous training program of shadowboxing, rope jumping, and one-on-one

George Mikan,
United Press International

Lone wolf Mikan in 1948, United Press International

Mikan shoots over New York in the 1953 NBA playoffs, United Press International

practice with a quick 5'6" guard. "As soon as George stopped feeling sorry for himself and realized his height was something to be admired," Coach Ray Meyer said, "he was on his way to being great."

Mikan was All-American each of his three years at DePaul, and twice was chosen the college player of the year. After he graduated in 1946, he joined the Chicago Gears for a record salary of $12,000. When the Gears folded at the end of that season, he began his astonishing career with the Minneapolis Lakers. In his first season, Mikan led the Lakers to the National Basketball League championship, averaging 21.3 points per game and earning unanimous recognition as the league's Most Valuable Player. His bulldozer approach to the basket was virtually unstoppable. Once, after a rival had accused him of rough play, Mikan ripped off his shirt to reveal a torso covered with black-and-blue marks, and growled, "What do you think these are—birthmarks?" His height, while making him a great popular draw, also made him a convenient target. He had lost four teeth in his first professional game and, as he said, "You've got to give it right back to them with a basket or a punch or they'll pound you right out of the league."

Mikan retired at the age of thirty, explaining that he wanted to quit, after the 1953–54 season, "at a peak of my career, while George Mikan is still George Mikan." He had not only revolutionized professional basketball with his style of play, but had lent it a popularity crucial to its formative years. In 1950, the Associated Press voted Mikan the basketball player of the half-century.

*Boston Celtics coach
Red Auerbach,* Russ
Adams, Photograph,
Sports Illustrated

RED AUERBACH (b. 1917)

For sixteen seasons, Coach Arnold "Red" Auerbach stormed the sidelines of the Boston bench, inciting the Celtics to ten National Basketball Association Eastern Division titles and nine world championships. He was selected to coach the NBA's All-Star game eleven consecutive years, from 1957 to 1967. As hot-tempered as his auburn hair suggests, Red Auerbach achieved the dubious distinction of accumulating more fines than any other NBA coach—a reputed $10,000 over the duration of his career. In the 1967 All-Star game, he was yanked out after thirty-four minutes and fined for allegedly swearing at the referee—the first time an All-Star coach had been ejected. But his pugnacious technique worked, and in the Boston Celtics he created a team which ranks with the Minneapolis Lakers as the best in professional basketball history.

Auerbach was born in what he calls a "not exactly genteel" section of Brooklyn, and played varsity basketball in high school. While not an enormously gifted natural player, he was highly motivated, and won a basketball scholarship to George Washington University, where he learned the fast-break maneuver which later became the hallmark of his own teams. During World War II, he organized and coached basketball teams in the Navy and, after the war, was hired to create a professional team in Washington, D.C. The "Capitols" finished first in their division in two out of their first three years, going all the way to the NBA championship finals in 1949 before losing to the Lakers.

In 1950, Auerbach was hired as head coach of the Boston Celtics, then moldering in the NBA Eastern Division cellar. He completely revamped the team and, in the 1950–51 season, the Celtics finished in second place. They dominated second place for five more years, until the arrival of center Bill Russell in 1956: from then on, the Celtics established themselves as the emperors of the courts. One sportswriter wrote in 1963 that "they play a different game from anyone else in the sport. It's more of a track meet than basketball." Their fleet, exhausting style of play demanded constant concentration on the court, a kind of mental freshness that was made possible by the depth of the team Auerbach had assembled. The Celtics had so many good players that it was said that he could just keep shuttling them in and out "until the opposition begins to feel like General Custer."

During the Celtics' reign, the irascible Auerbach was the NBA's leading personality as well as the preeminent coach. In 1956, he initiated his so-called "cigar ceremony," explaining, "When the league was pickin' on me, I tried to think of something that would aggravate the higher-ups. I wasn't having much luck until one day when I lighted up a cigar during a game. Afterwards I got a little note saying, 'It doesn't look good for you to be smoking cigars on the bench.' " He was never without one again.

Auerbach called himself a "compassionate dictator." He demanded discipline and superior conditioning from the players, because he was convinced that "through proper application you could make your body do a good deal more than it seemed capable of doing." It was this philosophy, along with a bone-jarring defense and a mastery of the fast break, which made the Auerbach-led Celtics the best—and the best-rewarded—team in basketball.

Auerbach with Mendy Rudolph, Jack O'Connell, Photograph, Boston Globe

Coach Red Auerbach with Bob Cousy and the Boston Celtics, United Press International

BOB COUSY (b. 1928)

In 1962 Bob Cousy was named the greatest all-around player in basketball history by a group of a hundred sports editors. During a career which lasted from 1950 to 1963, the 6′1½″ Cooz earned a reputation in basketball's Brobdingnagian world of seven-footers as "The Houdini of the Hardwood." A dazzling ball handler and playmaker, he changed the game, in the early days of professional basketball, from a shooting match among men with unstoppable shots into a technically more sophisticated and visually more interesting sport. Yet, when he showed up in 1950 to try out for the Boston Celtics, he was told by Coach Red Auerbach, "We need a big man. Little men are a dime a dozen." The coach never did pick Cousy on purpose—he picked his name out of a hat during a preseason National Basketball Association lottery. Years later, Auerbach admitted, "We got stuck with the greatest player in the league when we drew his name out of a hat."

As a college star at Holy Cross in Worcester, Massachusetts, Cousy earned a national reputation for his ball wizardry. It was at Holy Cross that he perfected such sleight-of-hand maneuvers as the behind-the-back dribble, the reverse dribble, and the behind-the-back pass.

Cousy, Boston's "Houdini of the Hardwood," Sports Illustrated ▶

Though relatively short, Cousy had ham-like hands, with large palms and extraordinarily long fingers that gave him a reach two inches longer than that of most men his size. His style of play was audacious, but his poise was arctic. He would plumb clogged courts open by draining off opposing players to one side of the court with his dribble, and then suddenly snake the ball behind his back to a teammate ninety degrees away. Only once did he use this flamboyance purposely to befuddle an opponent. In a game against the New York Knicks, Sweetwater Clifton seemed to be using his own razzle-dazzle ball handling not so much to play basketball as to make the Celtics look like fools. Cousy got mad and, dribbling up to Clifton, looked him in the eye and wound up as if to pitch a fastball right at him. Instead, he let the ball roll down his back into his left hand while he finished the "windmill" with his right arm and stuck his right hand toward Clifton with a "shake hands" gesture. It was an old Globetrotter trick. The fans loved it, though Cousy himself later said, "I shouldn't have done it but I was awfully sore at the time. . . . The next time we played New York I looked Clifton up and told him I was sorry about the incident, for I was. Clifton isn't a wise guy. He's a helluva nice guy. I should have taken that into account at the time."

Long captain of the Celtics, Cousy led them to five NBA championships. In one monumental effort—during the 1953 Eastern Division semifinal play-offs between the Celtics and the Syracuse Nats—he ripped in seventeen of the Celtics' last 21 points in a 111–105 victory that took four overtimes. Cousy scored 50 points—ten field goals, and a phenomenal thirty out of thirty-two free-throw attempts. After Bill Russell joined Cousy on the team in 1956, the Bostonians dominated basketball in much the same way as the Yankees ruled baseball. They won the championship in 1957, and in every year from 1959 through 1963. Cousy retired after that fifth championship and became a coach. But during their heyday, as Bill Russell has graciously said, "The image of the Celtics was the image of Bob Cousy."

Cousy seemingly defies the laws of gravity and centrifugal force as he flanks two would-be blockers, Hy Peskin, Photograph, 1956, Sports Illustrated

Bill Russell,
Robert Huntzinger,
Photograph, 1965,
Sports Illustrated

BILL RUSSELL (b. 1934)

"Defense is a science," Bill Russell once explained, "not a helter-skelter thing you just luck into. Every move has six or seven years of work behind it." When Russell began playing professional basketball in 1956, he brought systematic shot-blocking to the sport and transformed the underestimated science of rebounding into a fine art. No longer would crowds be content just to focus on how many times the ball fell into the hoop. What mattered increasingly, after Russell had entered the arena, was the defensive style—the finesse—that won games.

It has been said that it was a wonder that Russell ever became a basketball player at all. Even in high school, where as a sophomore he stood 6'2'' and weighed only 128 pounds, he was notably unsuccessful in sports until his senior year. "I should epitomize the American Dream," he once said, "for I came against long odds, from the farthest back to the very top of my profession. I came from the Depression. . . . I was not immediately good at basketball. It did not come easy." But when it came, it soared. He played well enough as a senior to win a scholarship to the University of San Francisco, a small Jesuit school with an unanswered prayer for a basketball team. By the 1954–55 and 1955–56 seasons, San Francisco was the top-ranked college basketball team in the country and the National Collegiate Athletic Association titleholder, and Bill Russell was the nation's number-one

Bob Cousy and Russell helped Boston dominate basketball from 1957 to 1963, Richard Meek, Photograph, Sports Illustrated

Bill Russell, Robert Handville, Mixed media, c. 1966, Collection of the artist

player. After graduating, he played on the gold-medal-winning U.S. Olympic basketball team at the 1956 games in Melbourne, Australia, and then signed with the Boston Celtics for $24,000.

In his first year as a professional, Russell provided the Celtics with the defensive dazzle they had been missing. With Russell in tandem with Bob Cousy, the team had an unbeatable one-two combination. They won the National Basketball Association championship that year and every year from 1958–59 to 1965–66. Cousy said of Russell that "he was the quickest big man in the league. Along with the intense desire and competitiveness and that unselfishness about him on the court, he had the instinct and reflexes and he wanted badly to be the best and keep us the best." Dubbed "The Eagle with a Beard," Russell could be arrogant and angry off court—"all hung up," Wilt Chamberlain once called him. *Sports Illustrated* lauded not just his physical prowess but "his admirable mind and purpose, his intelligence—he knows what to do with the ball—and his pride." He was named to the East All-Star team eleven times, and won the Most Valuable Player award five times. The dominating force in professional basketball during the 1960s, he was voted the basketball player of the decade by the Associated Press. Willis Reed has called Russell his boyhood idol: "He was the greatest."

After Cousy retired in 1963, Russell took over as the Celtics' captain. He proved a popular squad leader, and occasionally filled in as coach when Red Auerbach would be ejected from the bench. When Auerbach retired in 1966, Russell took over as the Celtics' new coach. The first black to be head coach of an NBA team, he was a playing coach until he retired in 1969—after he had led the Celtics to yet another championship.

227

◀ *Russell in a match with the New York Knicks,* James Drake, Photograph, 1969, Sports Illustrated

WILLIS REED (b. 1942)

For New York Knicks superstar Willis Reed, basketball was his ticket out of a small town in the red hills of northwestern Louisiana, where the only jobs for blacks, when he was growing up, were as field and mill hands. "I don't talk about things I don't know, but I know this," he said in 1971. "The basketball is a tool that the black has now, same as maybe once he had a plow. He can use it to make something of himself and make a life for his children."

In the eighth grade he turned his 6'2" body—too uncoordinated for a lot of sports— loose on a basketball court. "I wasn't good," he later admitted, "but I was big." He attended nearby Grambling College, a school noted for producing black professional football players, and became an All-American in basketball. The Knicks passed him up in the first round of the 1964 draft, but picked him in the second round. Phil Pepe, co-author of Reed's book *The View from the Rim*, has speculated that it was perhaps "the disappointment of not being selected on the first round that prompted Willis Reed to work hard to make it big in the NBA."

Reed himself says that he "came up aggressive" during his first pro season. One night, after the 6'8", 240-pound center had taken what he figured was the fiftieth elbow in his ribs without a foul being called, he exploded. When the dust settled, three of the five players of the opposing team were sprawled on the hardwood floor. One of Reed's teammates said, "Everything standing up was going down." After this incident, few players bothered him.

Reed's play, during his first season with the Knicks, netted him selection as the National Basketball Association Rookie of the Year. In the 1969–70 season, he led the team to its first championship. That season he was also voted Most Valuable Player—in the NBA, in the All-Star game, and in the play-offs. He won the MVP award again in 1973.

Probably the most important game of Reed's life came in the finals of the 1970 NBA play-offs between the Knicks and the Los Angeles Lakers, led by Wilt Chamberlain. He had been sidelined the entire sixth game by painful knee and hip injuries, and no one knew whether he would be able to play at all in the decisive seventh. No one, that is, but Reed. "For all my life, ever since I was 13 years old, that was where I wanted to be. I wanted to be playing . . . for a championship team." When it came down to the final game for the title, there "ain't no way in hell they gonna play that game without me. I got to go out there. Now, I don't know . . . if I can walk, but I got to go." If playing for the championship resulted in permanent injury which could end his career, so be it. "This is what I want."

Reed hobbled out, his knee and hip swelled by pain and Novocain, to play against the massive Chamberlain. Reed quickly put the first two shots of the game through the hoop, and then had to leave the court. But the Knicks were rocketed so high by his efforts that they virtually coasted to a 113–99 victory, and the first NBA championship in their history.

Teamwork was the keystone to Reed's ability. His Knick teammate Bill Bradley once summed him up as not the greatest technical center, nor the strongest rebounder or best defender. "But Willis blends his own skills . . . with the skills of . . . the rest of us, making each of us better and the team better and that's why he is, in fact, the best."

Willis, Joe Wilder, Oil on canvas, 1975, Spectrum Fine Art Gallery, New York City

WILT CHAMBERLAIN (b. 1936)

Wilt Chamberlain—"The Big Dipper"—made perhaps a greater impact on basketball than any other player. During a fourteen-year career that included play for the Harlem Globetrotters, Philadelphia's Warriors and 76ers, the San Francisco Warriors, and the Los Angeles Lakers, Chamberlain scored a phenomenal 30,000-plus points and pulled down 24,000 rebounds. When it comes right down to it, scoring is what basketball is all about—and "Wilt the Stilt" (a nickname he detests) was unparalleled at putting the ball through the hoop.

Born and raised in Philadelphia, Chamberlain was 6'11" by the time he went to high school. Basketball was not a burning passion with him, but he was so good at it that his career became almost inevitable. When he graduated in 1955, the owner of the Philadelphia Warriors got a special ruling from the National Basketball Association to allow him to claim Wilt as his first draft choice in 1959—since NBA rules then disallowed any player to compete in the league until the year his class graduated from college. Chamberlain played college basketball at the University of Kansas in Lawrence, which had outbid two hundred other schools for his services. During his sophomore and junior years, he led Kansas to forty-two wins in fifty games, and to second place in the National Collegiate Athletic Association tournament. He averaged 30 points per game and was named All-American both years. Then he became disenchanted with the four-man defense that opposing teams were using to keep him from the hoop. "I was guarded so closely that I thought I was going to spend the rest of my life looking out at the world through wiggling fingers, forearms, and elbows." Feeling that he wasn't getting the chance to develop his game, he turned professional after his junior year and joined the Harlem Globetrotters for the 1958–59 season. While waiting a year to be eligible to play for the Warriors, he earned $65,000 as a popular star with the Globetrotters. Then, beginning with the 1959–60 season, he joined the Warriors and proceeded to use his 7'2" and 300 pounds to dwarf nearly every professional basketball record in the book.

Chamberlain eventually broke eight of eleven records in his first NBA season: 37.6 average points per game; 2,707 points for the year; most field goals scored (1,065); and most rebounds (1,941). He was elected Rookie of the Year and the league's Most Valuable Player—the first time anyone had earned both awards in the same year.

Chamberlain revolutionized the sport by being "the most perfect instrument that God made to play basketball." Though not the first seven-footer to run down a basketball court, he was the most successful. When he leaped straight into the air for a basket, the top of his hand measured 13'3" from the floor. Before he began playing professional basketball, no one had seen the shattering slam-dunk he introduced to the sport—a shot which assured that basketball was henceforth to be a tall man's domain. He also demolished the ceiling on salaries from the moment he first signed with the Warriors, and proved that such an investment was worthwhile. Attendance rose greatly, and NBA franchises started to be big-time money-makers.

In a 1967 head-on match with Bill Russell and the Celtics for the NBA championship, Chamberlain put on one of the best performances of his career as the Philadelphia Warriors won their first world title from the Celtics. Afterward Russell strode into the enemy locker room, wearing his black cape, and sought out Chamberlain. "Great," was all he said.

◀ *Wilt Chamberlain in a quiet moment,* Richard Clarkson, Photograph, 1956, Collection of the photographer

Chamberlain finished his remarkable career with the Los Angeles Lakers, Walter Iooss, Jr., Photograph, 1972, Sports Illustrated

Wilt Chamberlain, Harold Castor, Polychromed bronze, c. 1971, Mr. and Mrs. Burton Cooper

Oscar Robertson, Russell Hoban, Oil on canvas, 1961, National Portrait Gallery, Smithsonian Institution. Gift of TIME, Inc.

OSCAR ROBERTSON (b. 1938)

Few players in the 1960s surpassed the all-around ability of "The Big O"—Oscar Robertson. Robertson grew up in an Indianapolis slum and learned to play basketball by heaving a rolled-up rag into a peach basket. At Crispus Attucks High School, he proved a sensation in a state which doted on basketball. He led his team to the first undefeated season in Indiana basketball history, and to two state championships. After graduating in 1956, he attended the University of Cincinnati, where he was chosen All-American three years in a row. From 1958 through 1960, he led the nation in scoring and, by the time he graduated, he had accumulated more points than any other player in college basketball history.

In the summer of 1960, following his graduation, Robertson co-captained the U.S. Olympic basketball team to an undefeated series and the world championship. Then, drafted by the cellar-ensconced Cincinnati Royals, he went on to a spectacular first professional season—a year in which he was selected Rookie of the Year for leading the National Basketball Association in assists and for coming in third in overall scoring. In that first season, the Royals' gross receipts tripled, and attendance soared. Then, in his sophomore year, Robertson took the Royals from the league basement to second place. Throughout the mid-1960s, he continued to spark Cincinnati to coming within reach of the title, but the team as a whole could never quite beat the Boston Celtics or the Philadelphia 76ers for the brass ring. The Big O, however, continued to rack up personal honors. He was consistently selected for the first string of the East–West All-Star game, and three times was voted that game's Most Valuable Player.

Quietly aggressive on the courts, Robertson got many of his shots by going one-on-one. He sleekly eased his 6'4½'' and 205 pounds around court rivals, threading the ball gracefully, tauntingly, toward the hoop. Another player once said, "If you give him a twelve-foot shot, Oscar will work on you until he's got a ten-foot shot. Give him ten, he wants eight. Give him eight, he wants six. Give him six, he wants four. Give him four, he wants two. Give him two, you know what he wants? . . . A lay-up."

Robertson was traded by the Royals to the newly franchised Milwaukee Bucks in 1970. During his first season with Milwaukee (1970–71), he joined Kareem Abdul-Jabbar to forge a combination considered to be the best big man–"little" man duo in the league. In their first season in tandem, they led the Bucks to a 66–16 record. In one stretch, they exploded for a record-winning streak of twenty games. This was also the season that The Big O finally got what had escaped him during a decade of professional basketball: a national championship, as the Bucks beat out the Baltimore Bullets for the 1971 NBA title.

It was the first and only professional championship team he ever played on. But, when he retired in 1974, Oscar Robertson was the highest-scoring guard of all time. He had a record total of 18,000 assists, and over 26,000 points—second in basketball history only to Wilt Chamberlain.

Robertson scoring against Texas Christian University, 1959, United Press International

JOHN WOODEN (b. 1910)

John Wooden is the only person to have been elected to the Basketball Hall of Fame for his accomplishments both as a player and as a coach. As an undergraduate at Purdue, he was known as "The India Rubber Man," since he was always careening around the court. A 5'10" guard, Wooden was called "suicidal" by *Time* magazine, because his drive for the basket "often sent him bouncing off the fieldhouse floor or flying into the seventh row of the Purdue band." According to a teammate, he "had a way of stalling the game by fantastic dribbling. He would dribble from backcourt to forecourt, all around, and nobody could get that ball away." From 1930 through 1932, he was three times All-American, and in 1932— the year Purdue had the national basketball championship team—he was also selected Player of the Year.

After serving in the U.S. Navy in World War II, Wooden coached at Indiana State Teachers College for two years before landing a permanent berth at the University of California at Los Angeles in 1948. The Bruins were then the weakest team in the Pacific Coast Conference, but during Wooden's first season they won twenty-two out of twenty-nine games. From then until his retirement in 1975, he never had a losing season. In his last twelve years, the Bruins won ten National Collegiate Athletic Association championships. During one phenomenal streak, covering the 1972–73 and 1973–74 seasons, they won eighty-eight games in a row. Wooden's overall record at UCLA was 620 victories and 147 losses—a winning percentage of .808.

As a coach, Wooden always insisted that the key to victory was defense, and he was considered the inventor of the full-court zone press—a sophisticated style of defense— which helped revolutionize college basketball in the 1960s. His players were highly conditioned. "The fast break is my system," he once said. "We'll win 50 percent of our games by out-running the other team in the last five minutes." But Wooden also put a lot of faith in inspirational coaching. At the start of each season, he would pass out copies of his "Pyramid of Success," a chart showing a pyramid cornerstoned on "industriousness" and "enthusiasm," strengthened by "faith" and "patience," and pinnacled by "success." It was a document perfectly in keeping with Wooden's status as a deacon in the First Christian Church. The silver-haired coach also instructed his players on the need for "mental, moral, and physical health." Wooden himself doesn't smoke, drink, or swear. When he is genuinely angry, "Saint John" is most likely to spew forth something on the order of "Goodness gracious sakes alive."

Although he has recruited and coached some of the greatest basketball players to hit the college courts, including Lew Alcindor (later Kareem Abdul-Jabbar) and Bill Walton, Wooden has based his success on solid overall coaching rather than dependence on a particular player. A rival coach credits Wooden's discipline and aggressive play-making for upsetting the tempo and style of his opposing team: "He does it by running, and running, and running some more. He mixes that up by hawking, by grabbing, by slapping, and by a hand-waving defense. His clubs dote on harassing the man with the ball."

By the time Wooden retired, in March 1975 (after UCLA had just won its tenth NCAA title), he had created a sports dynasty comparable to that of the New York Yankees or the Boston Celtics in their prime—and he had done it not by building success around a superstar or two whose careers would stretch over at least a decade, but with teams whose players never lasted longer than three years. With John Wooden, it was a case of the coach being greater than the sum of his starters.

John Wooden as a Purdue All-American, Basketball Hall of Fame, Springfield, Massachusetts

Coach Wooden during the razzle-dazzle of a UCLA game, Sheedy and Long, Photograph, 1972, Sports Illustrated

236

KAREEM ABDUL-JABBAR (b. 1947)

Perhaps the best center in basketball history, Kareem Abdul-Jabbar has dominated every court he has stepped on since he was twelve years old and 6'8". Born Lew Alcindor in New York City, he attended Power Memorial Academy, a Roman Catholic secondary school on Manhattan's West Side. There, he was carefully groomed by Coach Jack Donohue. "Most big boys are awkward," Donohue has recalled. "But after his freshman year, you couldn't say that about Lewie any more. Sure, he was given talent. But others have had that and didn't develop it. I think Lewie's biggest asset was tremendous pride."

The most sought-after high-school player in the country, Alcindor chose to go to the

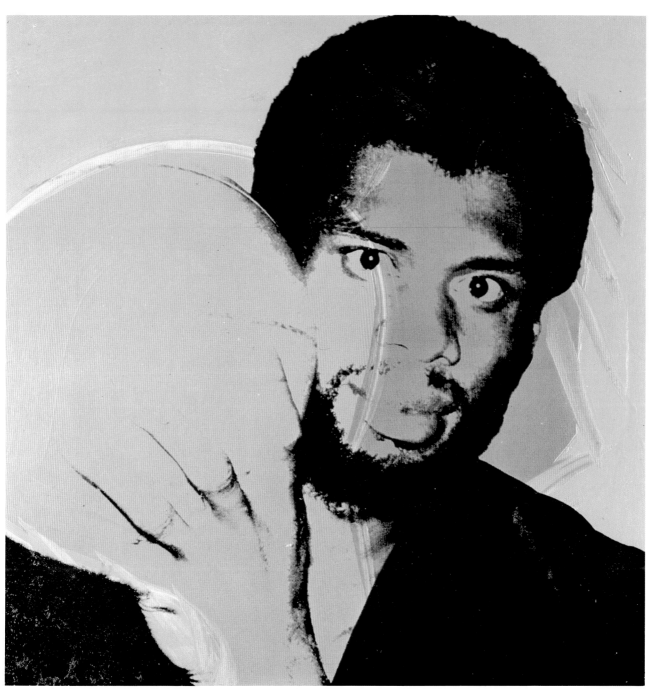

Kareem Abdul-Jabbar, Andy Warhol, Acrylic and silkscreen on canvas, 1979, Richard L. Weisman

University of California at Los Angeles and play under Coach John Wooden. In his first college game, he scored 31 points and led the UCLA freshmen to an astonishing 75–60 victory over the UCLA varsity—a team which had won the National Collegiate Athletic Association championship two out of the last three years. As one sportswriter said at the time, "UCLA is number one in the country and number two on its own campus." The next year, in his first game on the varsity, Alcindor scored 56 points as the Bruins crushed rival Southern California, 105–90. Even taciturn Coach Wooden was moved to describe Alcindor as "awesome." UCLA won all thirty of its games and the NCAA championship that year, and Alcindor was voted Most Valuable Player of the title tournament. In his junior and senior years, he led the Bruins to a record second, and then a third, consecutive national championship. It was in these last two years at UCLA that Alcindor became a Sunnite Muslim and took a new name, Kareem Abdul-Jabbar.

Signed by the Milwaukee Bucks for $1,400,000 in 1969, Abdul-Jabbar took the second-division Bucks—a new team which had won only twenty-seven games in the entire 1968–69 season—to fifty-six victories and the play-offs during his first National Basketball

Opposite:
Kareem Abdul-Jabbar and Bill Walton test their rivalry, Heinz Kleutmeier, Photograph, 1974, Sports Illustrated

Right:
Kareem Abdul-Jabbar taking a hook shot, Walter Iooss, Jr., Photograph, 1973, Sports Illustrated

Association year, 1969–70. He was second in the league in scoring, with a 28.8 average, and was selected Rookie of the Year. The next year, Oscar Robertson joined him on the Bucks, and the team became virtually unbeatable. Abdul-Jabbar led the NBA, with a scoring average of 31.7 in 1971–72, and, in the play-offs, the Bucks swept four straight games from the Baltimore Bullets to become world basketball champions. Kareem, who was voted the series' outstanding player, was asked by a fan, as he came off the courts, "Just like UCLA?" "No, no," he answered. "That was college. Here you're playing against the very best in the world." Named the NBA's Most Valuable Player for the first time that season, Abdul-Jabbar maintained the smooth, expressionless style of play identified with him. His only change was the addition of a healthy set of muttonchops and a pair of shatterproof goggles—a necessity after his eyes had been repeatedly gouged in this allegedly noncontact sport.

Traded to the Los Angeles Lakers, he continued to average more than 30 points per game—matching a record established by Wilt Chamberlain, the highest scorer in basketball history. Another champion, Bill Russell, has said that "Kareem Abdul-Jabbar will be remembered as the greatest center ever."

Bronco Buster (detail), N. C. Wyeth, Oil on canvas, 1907, The Minneapolis Institute of Arts, Gift of the National Biscuit Company

RODEO

Biography by
AMY HENDERSON

LARRY MAHAN (b. 1943)

Rodeo cowboys of an earlier era were as legendary for their way of life as for their way with broncs and bulls. It has been said that they would "arrive at a slumbering town, check in at the local saloon, wreck it, stagger off to the rodeo, ride their broncs, collect their winnings, and head right back to the saloon—and wreck the wreckage."

When Larry Mahan broke into professional rodeo at the age of sixteen, he was a fresh-faced, crew-cut youth with an easy grin. Nonsmoking and nondrinking, he came to represent a new brand of rodeo cowboy. "I've seen those old drunks," he said, "and that's not going to be me twenty years from now." And it wasn't, for during the course of his two-decade career, Mahan has done more to enhance the public image of the sport than any other figure. Along the way, he has also proved that rodeo can be big business. A financial expert who flies his own plane and has multi-faceted business interests, he has gone "from rides to riches" and is by far the wealthiest champion in rodeo history.

Born in Salem, Oregon, Mahan won his first rodeo prize at the age of twelve—six dollars and a belt buckle. After competing in youth rodeos, he joined the Professional Rodeo Cowboys Association (PRCA) in 1963 and posted his first professional win in bull riding. Of the six main events in rodeo—team roping, individual calf roping, steer wrestling, saddle bronc, bareback bronc, and bull riding—Mahan is a champion in the last three, an unparalleled achievement in this sport of specialists. Bull riding has held a particular fascination for him: "On a horse you can sometimes make a mistake and pick up in time to save yourself, but a

Larry Mahan showing the style that made him six-time All-Around Champion Cowboy,
Fred Kaplan, Photograph, 1973, Sports Illustrated

Mahan is dragged at the Ellensburg (Washington) Rodeo, John P. Foster, Photograph, 1971, Collection of the photographer

Mahan between events, Prorodeo Hall of Champions and Museum of the American Cowboy, Colorado Springs, Colorado

bull usually won't give you a second chance." The moment of truth comes when a rider eases himself onto the bull's broad back in the chutes and takes his grip on the rope. Mahan says, "Sometimes you find yourself wishing there was an honorable way to get out of what you're about to do." He puts his gloved right hand through the grip in the rope noosed around the bull's neck, and another cowboy—a "rigger"—cinches it tight and wraps it once more around the gloved hand. When Mahan yells that he's ready, the bull is turned out, and a savage contest of wills begins. Mahan has been seriously injured by these wild-eyed Brahmas four times, the first of which came while he was still in high school. He broke his jaw badly, and admits to having "a few chickens in my gas tank after that." But "you forget about the bad things."

Success in the sport depends not only on rhythm, balance, and guts, but on mental attitude. "You have to become very aggressive," he has said. "You have that desire to get out there and win." Fear plays a part in it, "but after you reach a certain point of professionalism, you can overcome that. I know when I ride . . . I'm really hyped up, and I'm into a totally different world." Winning is "to me what alcohol is to the alcoholic. . . . I've got to have it."

Mahan won his first PRCA World All-Around championship in 1966, and successfully defended his title in 1967, 1968, 1969, 1970, and—after being plagued with injuries in 1971 and 1972—again won in 1973. He was the first ever to compete in three events (bull, bareback, and saddle bronc riding) and, in the national finals, where a rider has to compete in his events eight different times in six days, he had to come out of the chutes a remarkable twenty-four times. The word on the rodeo circuit is that he has adrenal glands the size of cantaloupes. His sense of dramatic flair and his dash have made him a virtual folk hero— "the apotheosis," an admirer once said, "of the new breed of rodeo cowboys."

At the Crease, Ken Danby, Egg tempera, 1972, Private collection through Gallery Moos, Toronto

ICE HOCKEY

Biographies by
AMY HENDERSON

GORDIE HOWE (b. 1928)

For thirty-two seasons, Gordie Howe played "religious hockey"—his description of a sport in which it is better to give than to receive. Howe's professional career ultimately spanned an incredible five decades, beginning in the mid-1940s and ending in 1980. He retired for the first time in 1971, at the age of forty-three, after twenty-five years and 1,841 games with the Detroit Red Wings. A rival has said of Howe that he was "everything you'd expect an ideal hockey player to be. He's soft-spoken and thoughtful. He's also the most vicious, cruel, and mean man I've ever met in a hockey game."

Howe was born in Saskatchewan, on the outskirts of Canada's wheat-farming country. "When I played goalie," he once recalled, "I used to skate a mile from my house to the rink, holding pads up in front of me to cut the wind. At one rink they had a heated shack. A guy would ring a cowbell and the forward lines and the defense for both teams would go off and sit in the shack by the potbellied stove to warm up while the alternates played." By the time he was sixteen, Gordie was scouted regularly by professional teams. In 1945, he signed with Omaha and played there for a year before going to the Detroit Red Wings. After two unspectacular seasons with Detroit, he suddenly caught fire and scored 35 goals and 33 assists for 68 points—only to finish off the year with a near-fatal accident.

It happened during the 1950 Stanley Cup play-offs. Howe was skating at full force when he collided with Ted Kennedy of the Toronto Maple Leafs. He fractured his skull, cheekbone, and nose, and suffered a lacerated right eye. And he spent three hours undergoing life-saving brain surgery. The accident left him with a compulsive eye-blinking tick and a nickname, "Blinkie."

Though it was questionable for a time whether Howe could ever return to the ice, he was back the next season, and in supreme style. He scored 43 goals and 43 assists in 1950–51, to emerge as the leading scorer in the NHL with 86 points. For three more seasons, he would be the league's top scorer, and five times—1952, 1953, 1957, 1958, and 1960—he won the coveted Hart trophy as the NHL's outstanding player.

Howe was built to play hockey. Six feet tall and 205 pounds, he had enormous upper body strength in his prime. With his huge hands and strong wrists, he could flick a wrist shot at 114 mph. The wrist shot is the game's most deadly, and Howe could make it with either hand. He used a special twenty-one-ounce stick with an exceptionally stiff handle. The Red Wing trainer said, "Give Gordie a stick with an ordinary handle and he'll break it like a toothpick. He is so strong that when he shoots, that handle bends like a banana."

Howe was a tireless skater, with a pulse rate of 48. From 1957 to 1964, he played an average of forty to forty-five minutes per sixty-minute game, or nearly twice the time of most forwards. He was also a subtle, treacherous skater who could collapse opponents by throwing elbow shots so rhythmically that they were invisible. He rarely got caught, but one of the most memorable times when he did was in 1965, just after he had scored his six-hundredth goal. The usually hostile Montreal crowd gave Red Wing Howe a standing ovation, and had barely returned to their seats when old "Number 9" had them up again, but this time they were screaming for his head. Howe had gone after a Canadien defenseman, and got a stiff five-minute penalty. The Canadien got a broken cheekbone.

Gordie Howe retired from the Red Wings in 1971, but was soon back playing for the World Hockey League Houston Aeros. In 1977, he joined the Hartford Whalers. He has said that the peak of his career came with the Whalers, where two of his teammates were his sons, Marty and Mark. Finally, in 1980, Gordie Howe—fifty-two years old and two times a grandfather—retired. In thirty-two seasons, he had set records for most goals scored (1,071), most games played (2,421), and most assists (1,518). "I'm going to miss it," he said as the Whalers retired his Number 9 jersey. "I'd be rock hard if I didn't."

◀ *Gordie Howe, still playing at forty-five,* Neil Leifer, Photograph, 1974, Sports Illustrated

Bobby Orr of the Boston Bruins,
Neil Leifer, Photograph, 1970,
Sports Illustrated

Opposite:
*Orr after scoring the goal that
won the Stanley Cup for the Bruins
in 1970,* Ray Lussier, Photograph,
Wide World Photos, Inc.

BOBBY ORR (b. 1948)

Bobby Orr was signed to an amateur contract by the Boston Bruins when he was fourteen.
Sent to the Oshawa Generals in the Junior A division of the Ontario Hockey Association,
he was four or five years younger than most of the other players, and weighed only 125
pounds. By the time he was eighteen and eligible to turn professional, Bobby Orr had already
become something of a legend. In 1966, when he signed with the Bruins for $41,000—the
most lucrative rookie contract ever in the National Hockey League—he was touted in
Boston as the player who could lead the team out of their basement wallow. It was a hefty
burden for the shy, deferential eighteen-year-old, and Orr admits to having been "a little
nervous about the reaction among the Bruins" before the start of his first training camp. But
the team embraced him, and one astonished teammate—after watching Orr flash impressively
down the rink—told him, "I don't know what you're getting [paid], kid, but it isn't enough."

In the wake of all the hoopla to promote his debut in the pros, Orr said that he was
more worried than he had ever been in his life. "This was what I was waiting for. The
NHL." He was greeted warmly in his first games by juggernaut opponents like Gordie Howe,
who walloped him with a two-handed swat. Soon young Bobby started to hit back. After
knocking the pins from under some of the toughest players in the league, he got his message
across. "I don't look for fights," he said, "but I don't back down from them either."

Orr's rookie season was as sensational as the promotional ballyhoo had predicted.
Boston crowds went into a frenzy of total adoration, and even his coach called him "a star
from the moment they played the National Anthem in his first NHL game." He won the
Calder Trophy as the Rookie of the Year and, over the next three years, forged the Bruins
into a championship team. They won the Stanley Cup in 1970 and 1972 and, in both years,

Orr was awarded the Conn Smythe Trophy as the outstanding player in the Cup series.

Characterized by sportswriters as a "magician" and a "hot-rodder" with "eighteen speeds of fast," Orr always said that he succeeded because he "looked for the opening. If it's there, I take it. If it's not I get rid of the puck." He won the Hart Memorial Trophy as the league's Most Valuable Player a record three times in succession, and the Norris Trophy five times as the league's top defenseman. He also set records for goals by a defenseman, and for assists by any player. In fact, Orr accomplished what no other defenseman had ever done: he became his team's major scoring threat, and thereby changed the scope of the game. Unlike a forward such as Gordie Howe, Orr as a defenseman would start from the far end of the rink, away from the offensive action. Then, after waiting in the reeds, he would sweep in and score with bullet-like wrist shots from short range. Another player described how Orr trailed the play: "He never has to rush up unless he wants to. He can pick his spots. He can wait until the end of a shift. The players have been on the ice for two minutes while he's been laying back. . . . Orr gets the puck and just leaves those guys behind him because they are too tired to catch up. He could beat them anyway."

Even when he was plagued by knee problems—as he was during the 1972 Stanley Cup series—Orr remained a stealthy, seemingly effortless skater. At 5′11″ and 175 pounds, he was lighter than most defenders. He was also an instinctive playmaker. To his Boston coach, he was "the greatest player there's ever been." Finally, with his knees giving out, Orr was traded to the Chicago Black Hawks in 1976 for $600,000. After seven knee operations, though, he called it quits. Orr said that if he couldn't play his best anymore he wouldn't play at all. Gracious to the end, he never cashed a single Chicago paycheck.

BOBBY HULL (b. 1939)

In his prime as a Chicago Black Hawk during the 1960s, Bobby Hull was the biggest name in hockey. Enormously popular with crowds, the ruggedly handsome "Golden Boy"— so-called because of his choirboy blond curls—could seemingly shoot a goal at his pleasure. The fastest skater in the National Hockey League, he was once clocked at 28.3 mph skating with the puck, and at 29.7 mph without it.

Bobby Hull was raised on his parents' farm in Ontario, the fifth child and oldest son among eleven children. "Saturday night was hockey night," he once recalled, "and our whole family would gather round the radio to hear . . . the game from Maple Leaf Gardens." He started skating at the age of three and, by the time he was twelve, was a member of his father's team in an intermediate league. Years of chopping wood and doing strenuous farm chores had given him a bull-like physique that would later lead a Chicago society-page columnist to gush that he was "a statue come alive from the Golden Age of Greece, incredibly handsome even without his front teeth."

In 1957, Hull was signed by the Chicago Black Hawks. Only eighteen, he played at center for his first two seasons; but then, switched to left wing, he began to soar. In 1959–60, Hull led the NHL with 39 goals; in 1961–62, he scored 50 goals—a record he shattered in 1965–66 with 54 goals, and in 1968–69 with 58. He was selected for the All-Star team twelve of his fourteen years in the league and, at the end of the 1960s, the Associated Press voted him player of the decade.

Blurring speed was what set Bobby Hull apart. He could slap a puck at speeds of 120 mph, nearly 35 mph faster than the average hockey player and, in fact, faster than anyone else who had ever played the game. An opponent who was hit by one of his shots and lived to tell about it has said, "When Hull winds up and lets fly, that puck comes at you like a small town." Another player has observed that "compared to his shots, others are tennis balls." One, who had stopped a sixty-foot slap shot, said, "It felt like I had been seared by a branding iron. His shot once paralyzed my arm for five minutes. It's unbelievable!"

In 1971–72, Hull had his fourth 50-goal season. He retired from the NHL that year with a career total of 604 goals. "Every day the game loses some of its appeal," he lamented. "Expansion has diluted the old pride that gave such prestige to playing in a six-team, one-hundred-twenty-man league." Ironically, expansion of the league had come about because of the burgeoning popularity of the sport—for which Hull himself was partially responsible.

Hull's retirement had lasted but a few weeks when he signed a contract for $2,750,000, in June of 1972, to become player-coach for Winnipeg in the new World Hockey Association. He scored more than 50 goals five more times in his career, and his total of 1,012 goals was second only to Gordie Howe's record. He retired in 1978, after twenty-two seasons and 1,447 games, the richest hockey player ever.

◀ *Bobby Hull,* Neil Leifer, Photograph, 1967, Sports Illustrated, Collection of the photographer

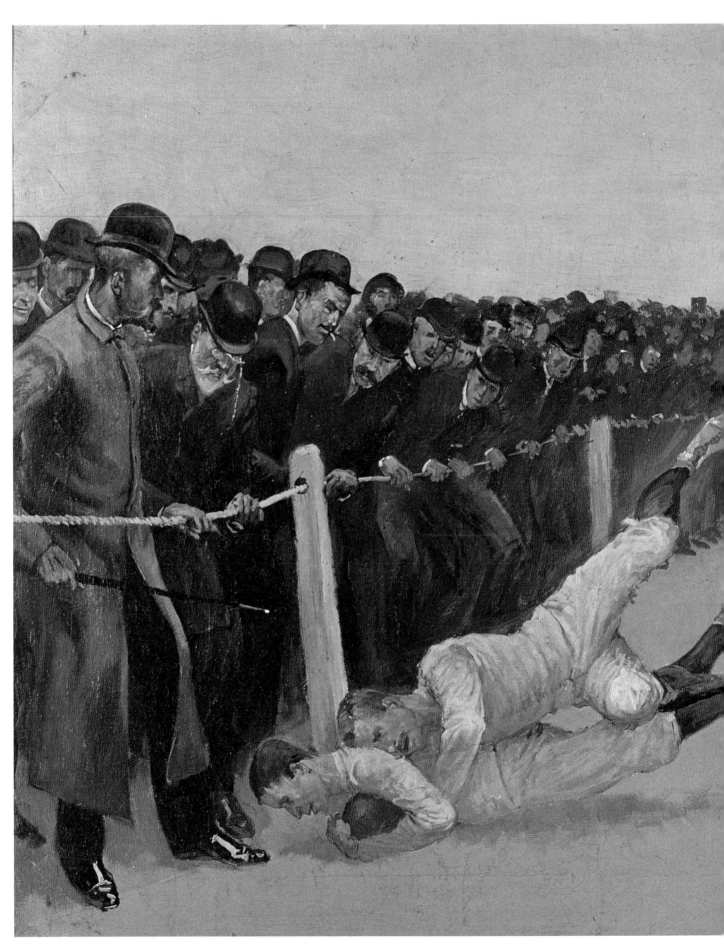

Touchdown, Yale vs. *Princeton, Thanksgiving Day, November 27, 1890, Yale 32, Princeton 0,* Frederic Remington,
Oil on canvas, 1890, Yale University Art Gallery, Whitney Collection of Sporting Art

FOOTBALL

Biographies by
MARGARET CHRISTMAN

Forward Pass, Thomas Hart Benton, Oil on canvas, 1971, Lyman Field and United
Missouri Bank of Kansas City, Trustees, Thomas Hart Benton Testamentary Trusts

Football Players, Duane Hanson, Polyester resin and fiberglass, 1969, Neue Galerie, Aachen, West Germany

WALTER CAMP (1859–1925)

To Walter Camp belongs the title of "Father of American Football." For forty-eight years, beginning during his undergraduate years at Yale, Camp served on every football rules committee or attended every football convention from 1878 until his death in 1925. No one was more influential in shaping the slowly evolving sport.

When Camp began to play football for Yale in America's centennial year, the game was still in a primitive state, characterized most often by the word "brutality." Played with a rugby-shaped ball on an open field where pieces of clothesline took the place of crossbars, the red-meat game was replete with fisticuffs among the players. It was common practice to jump crushingly upon the opponent in the frank hope of immobilizing him.

Camp played six years for Yale, continuing, as the rules of eligibility then allowed, after he had entered the Medical School. In an era when kicking was the prime feature of the sport, Camp was noted for his abilities to drop-kick on the run from as far out as thirty-five yards. He also played defensive tackle. It was said that "he may be small, but he's all spirit and whipcord."

In 1878, as captain of his college team, Camp attended his first rules committee meeting. He recommended that the number of players be reduced from fifteen to eleven, a change which was finally agreed to in 1880. Camp proposed, and got speedily adopted, the

The award given to Camp for "Longest Run—90 Yards," 1880, The Sports Immortals Museum Collection, Joel Platt, Director

Left:
Walter Camp, "Father of American Football," Janet Camp Troxell

Camp (holding the ball), *with Yale University football team, 1879. The artist*
Frederic Remington is seated at far right, Yale University Archives, Yale University Library

regulation that a team must gain five yards in three downs to keep the ball, a stipulation later altered to ten yards in four downs. Asked how he proposed to tell when five yards had been made, Camp replied, "We shall have to rule off the field with horizontal chalked lines every five yards." "Gracious!" was the reply, "the field will look like a gridiron!" "Precisely," said Camp.

Thanks to Camp, who continued as an unpaid adviser, Yale dominated football's early years and, before he retired from the college in 1910, he had trained a whole generation of coaches. Rival teams joked that "no one could expect to beat Yale since Camp had made up the rules of the game." Nonetheless, nobody ever questioned his fairness; Camp's sportsmanship was unimpeachable.

In the mid-1890s, at a time when bad feeling created a hiatus in the Harvard–Yale contest, Camp collaborated with Lorin F. Deland, head coach at Harvard, in writing the first complete book on the game of American football. Following his retirement from Yale, Camp authored several more treatises on the sport as well as on physical education in general. In 1889, initially with journalist Caspar Whitney, he began his lifelong task of selecting an All-American team. The list, published in *Colliers'* magazine, did much to advertise football nationally.

Immediately after Camp's death, which came while he was attending the annual meeting of the football rules committee, there was a spontaneous desire from schools and colleges all over the country for a memorial in his honor. Two hundred twenty-five universities and colleges and 279 preparatory and high schools contributed to a gateway, erected at the entrance of the Yale athletic field, "To Honor Walter Camp and the Traditions of American College Sport Which He Exemplified."

Glenn "Pop" Warner (left) *and Jim Thorpe reminisce about their years at Carlisle, 1931,* United Press International

Warner as a Cornell guard in 1894,
United Press International

POP WARNER (1871–1954)

Glenn S. ("Pop") Warner, who had one of the most inventive minds in the history of football, is remembered for many innovations, including the crouch start, the single and double wingback formations, and improvements in protective field equipment for the players in the way of thigh and shoulder padding developed from a lightweight fiber. Warner, who began to play the game in what he called the era of "tousled hair and overpadded pants," was the first to bring colorful uniforms to the field when, in 1924, he outfitted the Stanford team in pants of red rather than the traditional khaki color. "I was fortunate to be coaching in the early days," Warner said, "when football was having growing pains and it was not then difficult to see how the game and equipment could be improved."

Pop Warner's coaching career spanned forty-six years, and in that time he developed many fine teams and a galaxy of individual stars, forty-seven of whom were declared All-American. His first great protégé was Jim Thorpe, whom he coached at the tiny Indian school in Carlisle, Pennsylvania. Superintendent R. H. Pratt had asked Walter Camp to recommend the foremost young coach in the country. Warner, who had coached the University of Georgia to an undefeated season and who had had additional experience off-season at Iowa State College, was hired at the unheard-of salary of $1,200. Under Warner, football became big business at Carlisle. His teams, which played most of the time on the road, taking the measure of almost every big university in the country, traveled as far as California and raised large sums of money for the school.

The teams were so small that Warner had no more than two or three substitutes. Every player had to be able to play several positions, and all were trained to kick. Carlisle was invariably outweighed by the opposition, but they specialized in trick plays. The most celebrated of the wily stratagems was the "hunchback play" used against Harvard in 1907. The ball, kicked high and deep by Harvard, was picked up by the Carlisle receiver, who was concealed behind a broad V-formation. Deftly the receiver stuffed the ball up the back of a jersey which had been reinforced with elastic bands to prevent a fumble. As Harvard scrambled frantically after Carlisle players running with their helmets cradled under arm, the Carlisle receiver ran 103 yards for a touchdown, pulling the ball from his jersey just at the goal line. As it turned out, the deception infuriated Harvard to a vengeance that resulted in two touchdowns that won the game for Harvard, 12–11. Nonetheless, the public was entranced, and the play lived for years in vaudeville and the movies.

Pop remained at Carlisle until 1914, when a Congressional investigation called for a de-emphasis on football and recommended his dismissal. Among the charges placed against the coach was profanity, although the hard-swearing Warner had tried to curb it since he knew that the Indians took personal offense. Warner went on to coach at Pittsburgh for nine seasons, producing three undefeated teams, with the 1916 squad rated as one of the all-time best. At Stanford he coached three Rose Bowl teams. At Temple he took the team to the first Sugar Bowl.

In the years after World War I, all of football was divided into two camps—advocates of the shift formation practiced by Knute Rockne, and advocates of the double wingback which Warner first introduced when Stanford played Notre Dame at the Rose Bowl game in 1925. Notre Dame won, 27–10, but the following year, when Stanford defeated California, 27–14, the Warner system proved its effectiveness. The East discovered the double wing during the 1928 game when Stanford tore through Army at will, winning 26–0, and making Pop Warner the coach of the hour.

Amos Alonzo Stagg's coaching career spanned seventy years, Bettmann Archive, Inc.

Opposite:
Stagg talking to football candidates at the University of Chicago, Library of Congress

AMOS ALONZO STAGG (1862–1965)

Amos Alonzo Stagg, "The Grand Old Man of American Football," first came to the game during Yale's glory years, when the school's football success was compared to a righteous life—"monotonous but satisfying." Stagg was a member of the great 1888 team, captained by William H. "Pa" Corbin, which, in a season of thirteen games, scored 698 points and left their opponents with nothing at all. Stagg, who concentrated on baseball during his undergraduate years, finally turned to football while a theological student. Teammate William W. "Pudge" Heffelfinger, one of the greatest guards to play the game, remembered, "For all his biblical precepts, Lon was the foxiest of gridiron tacticians. He thought two plays ahead of the other fellow, like a master surveying a chessboard." Both Stagg and Heffelfinger were members of the first All-American team, selected in 1889.

Deciding that he didn't speak well enough in public to be a successful minister, Stagg enrolled at Springfield College to prepare for a career in physical education, and was then hired as head of the physical education department at the University of Chicago in 1892. An athletic field was nonexistent. Stagg got a fence built around a vacant lot for baseball games in time to attract the crowds attending the nearby World's Columbian Exposition; and he used the profits to subsidize his athletic program. The field, named in his honor in 1914, was, to his great dismay, torn down in 1957 after the University of Chicago gave up intercollegiate football. During Stagg's forty-one seasons at Chicago, his football teams won six Western Conference titles and tied for another. Stagg coached five undefeated teams.

After Stagg reached Chicago's mandatory retirement age of seventy, he went on to the College of the Pacific in Stockton, California, where he coached for fourteen more years.

With the help of experienced players sent to Pacific in the World War II program for officer training, the college of less than six hundred students became a football power capable of defeating both the University of California at Berkeley and the UCLA teams.

When he was eighty-nine, Stagg stepped aside as head coach, but went on to Susquehanna College, where he served as his son's co-coach. He handled the offense until 1952, when he went back to Stockton to serve as an adviser at the Junior College. In 1960, at the age of ninety-eight, he said, "I guess it's about time to quit. I have already coached for 70 years—63 in which I was the whole works practically." Stagg had presided over more winning football games than any other coach, edging out Pop Warner by one.

Stagg was remarkable, not only for his longevity but also for his many contributions to the game. "All football comes from Stagg," said Knute Rockne. Speaking of the line shift, out of which developed what came to be called the Notre Dame shift, Rockne said, "I got it from Jesse Harper [University of Chicago player under Stagg and predecessor of Rockne at Notre Dame], who got it from Stagg, who got it from God."

Stagg's teams were taught to block and tackle hard. He also demanded clean play and clean language. He himself never swore, although he sometimes called a player a jackass and, under extreme provocation, a double jackass. Stagg believed in football as a sport and also as a character-builder. In *Touchdown*, a book he wrote in 1927, he proclaimed: "To me, our profession is one of the noblest and perhaps the most far reaching in building up the manhood of our country." Winning, he said, "isn't worthwhile unless one has something finer and nobler behind it. When I reach the soul of one of my boys with an idea or an ideal or a vision, then I think I have done my job as a coach."

Knute Rockne,
United Press International

Rockne exercising his men,
National Portrait Gallery,
Smithsonian Institution

KNUTE ROCKNE (1888-1931)

Knute Rockne, said a Notre Dame alumnus, "sold football to the men on the trolley, the elevated, the subway . . . the baker, the butcher, the pipe fitter who never went to college. He made it an American mania. He took it out of the thousand-dollar class and made it a million-dollar business." Rockne, who planned the season's schedule with an eye to the places where he could draw the best crowds, took on formidable teams from all over the country. Notre Dame played before almost one million spectators each year and lost only twelve games in the thirteen years Rockne was the head coach. Five times they had undefeated seasons; six times they went down but once. Never was there a losing year.

Rockne's success begat success. Notre Dame had no trouble recruiting the top high-school players. During one season, there were more than thirty high-school captains on the freshman squad. In turn, Notre Dame alumni were in demand as coaches. At the time of Rockne's death, twenty-three of his boys were head coaches at colleges, dozens of others were assistant coaches, and at least 150 were coaching at the high-school level.

A master of psychology, Rockne once wrote, "A team in an ordinary frame of mind will do only ordinary things. In the proper emotional stage, a team will do extraordinary things. To reach this stage, a team must have a motive that has an extraordinary appeal to them." The guileful Rockne was never at a loss when it came to motivation—his little boy, he once told the team, begged for a win before he died of pneumonia. In fact, the child was perfectly well. Rockne himself, when felled by phlebitis, was carried into the locker room to plead for a win and then, he pronounced, "Let the blood clot move where it may." The most legendary moment of all came when he exhorted his boys to "win this one for the old Gipper." This Rockne used in 1928, his poorest season, when Notre Dame was threatened by Army, the nation's number-one team. At half time Rockne related the last words of George Gipp, the dazzling halfback who had died of a streptococcus infection eight years earlier. "Some day, Rock, when the team's up against it; when things are wrong and the breaks are beating the boys—tell them to go in there with all they've got and win just one for the Gipper." Army was vanquished, 12–6.

Adam Walsh, captain of the Notre Dame team in 1924, recalled: "As a coach Rockne was tough as hell—a real taskmaster, but he was a perfectionist as tough on himself as on his men. He was devoted to his men and had their confidence and respect, their affection." Out of deference for Rockne, who scorned the professional game, Walsh and the coordinated backfield, immortalized by Grantland Rice as "The Four Horsemen"—Harry Stuhldreher, Don Miller, Jim Crowley, and Elmer Layden—turned down George Halas's offer to play for the Chicago Bears.

Rockne, the only nonperformer of the 1920s sports heroes, became one of the best-known personalities in America. He wrote books and magazine articles; he ran coaching clinics; he was in constant demand as an after-dinner speaker. The Studebaker company hired him to give inspirational talks to their salesmen and executives. Rockne's death, in the crash of a small plane, stunned the country. Will Rogers gave voice to the public emotion: "We are becoming so hardened by misfortune and bad luck that it takes a mighty big calamity to shock this country. But, Knute, you did it. We thought it would take a president's death to make a whole nation shake their heads in real sorrow and say, 'Ain't it a shame he's gone?' Well, that's what this country did today, Knute, for you. You died one of our national heroes."

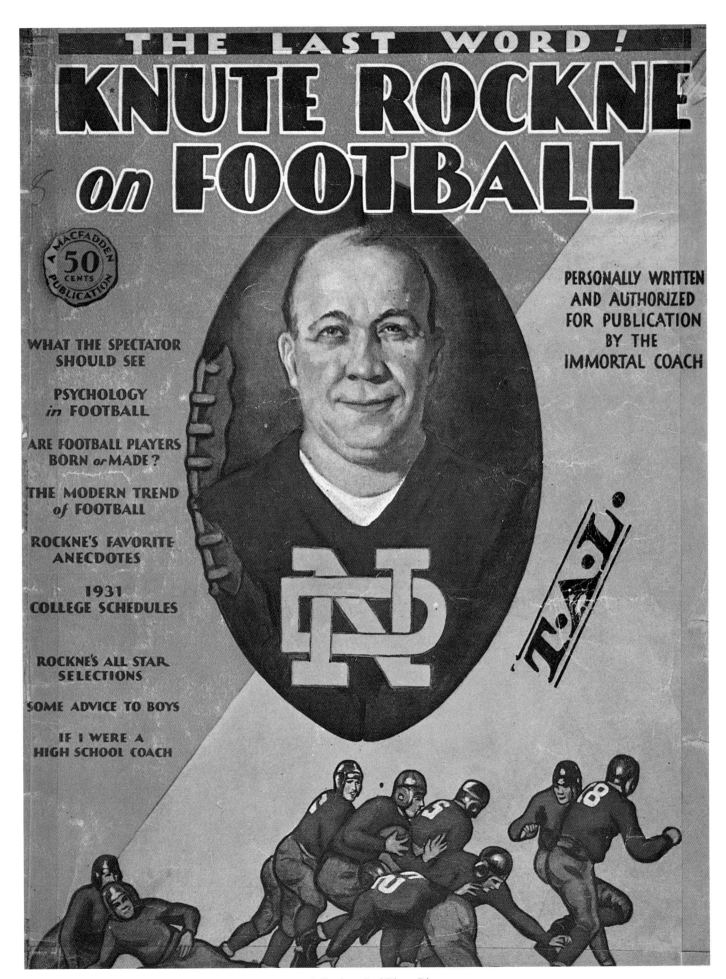

A Notre Dame magazine, The Sports Immortals Museum Collection, Joel Platt, Director

RED GRANGE (b. 1903)

On October 18, 1924, "a tall greyhound of a boy, with hair the color of a sunset," flashed to national attention in a football game played at the dedication of the University of Michigan's Memorial Stadium. Red Grange, a sophomore at the University of Illinois, ran the opening kickoff back ninety-five yards for a touchdown and followed up, during the next ten minutes, with three more. Grange added one more touchdown in the second half, and passed for yet another. Michigan, a team unvanquished during the preceding three seasons, went down, 39–14.

Dubbed "The Galloping Ghost," Grange became the most publicized football player in the Golden Age of American Sport. His broken-field running, his ability to dodge, weave, twist, glide, and change pace, left his would-be tacklers far behind. "Grange runs as . . .

Chicago Bears star Red Grange, Bettmann Archive, Inc.

Official Foot-Ball Program 1926

"77"

"77"

Chicago Bulls Football Club *vs.* "Red" Grange's New York Yankees

Sunday, October 17, 1926 — 2:15 P. M.

Comiskey Park

Price **10** Cents

An official football program, 1926, International Sports and Games Research Collection, University of Notre Dame Libraries

Opposite:
"The Galloping Ghost" of the gridiron, Library of Congress

Dempsey moves, with almost no effort, as a shadow flits and drifts and darts," wrote Grantland Rice. Americans were entranced, and flocked to buy radios so as not to miss their hero's latest Saturday-afternoon exploit.

Red was a senior before the somewhat skeptical East got to see what the Midwest had known for three years, that he was, as the Chicago *Tribune* put it, "the greatest football player of the decade." In the first five minutes of play against the mighty University of Pennsylvania team, he ran fifty-five yards on a slippery, muddy field, and there was not a man within twenty-five yards of him when he crossed the goal line. From then on, "There goes the Redhead!" was the incessant chant. When, near the end of the second quarter, Grange was called out for a breathing spell, the *Tribune* reported: "With one spontaneous, beautifully sportsmanlike motion 63,000 human beings rose to their feet in tribute to the lad walking slowly through the seas of mire."

The popular hero did the unthinkable, in the eyes of many—including his coach, Bob Zuppke—when he brought his enormous prestige to the cause of professional football. On November 22, 1925, the day after he had played his last college game, Grange signed a contract, negotiated by his manager, Charles C. Pyle, guaranteeing him at least $100,000 to play with George Halas's and Dutch Sternaman's Chicago Bears. That Grange's name was magic to the generally ignored professional game was obvious when on Thursday next, Thanksgiving Day, a capacity crowd of 36,000 turned out at Wrigley Field. College games of the time might draw 40,000 to 50,000 spectators, but the professionals were lucky to

attract 10,000 customers even when Jim Thorpe, now in his declining years, was advertised. In the promotional tour which followed, Grange, traveling with the eager sportswriters in tow, played seventeen games between December 24 and January 31. Before it was over, 400,000 fans had paid to see him play, and for the first time the South, and the East and West coasts, had been exposed to professional football.

Under the management of "C.C." ("Cash and Carry," he was dubbed) Pyle, Grange became the first of the marketable football celebrities. He endorsed Red Grange dolls, a sweater, a cap just like the one he wore, a ginger ale, a candy bar, and even a meat loaf. Sportswriters were frankly asked to submit ideas for a script on which Grange could "ride to fame on the silver screen." He starred in the successful *One Minute to Play* in 1926, and in 1929 played himself in a talkie, *The Galloping Ghost*.

Grange and Pyle started their own league in 1927, but it was a financial failure and lasted only a year. George Halas persuaded Grange to return to the Bears in 1929; he continued to play until 1935 and after that stayed on as assistant coach for several more seasons. In the professional league—up against stiffer competition than in the amateur sport, and slowed down by a 1927 knee injury—Grange's career was not as glittering as it had been at Illinois. But, even as he lost some of the speed of his legendary years and was not able to break away for the fabled long runs, Grange developed into a first-class blocker and a fine defensive halfback. Most important, however, he brought to professional football respectability, and its first surge of popularity.

Bronko Nagurski, The Sports Immortals
Museum Collection, Joel Platt, Director

Left:
Nagurski in 1936, Chicago Historical Society

BRONKO NAGURSKI (b. 1908)

If football can be said to have a truly mythic figure, that figure is Bronko Nagurski. Coach Doc Spears of the University of Minnesota discovered him, so the story goes, when he asked directions of a boy plowing the fields at International Falls—without a horse. Nagurski responded by pointing the way—with the plow.

At Minnesota, the strong farmboy played tackle and fullback and was chosen All-American in both categories. During one college game, he performed as end, tackle, guard, halfback, and fullback. His coach declared that he could have been All-American at any one of the five positions.

Upon Nagurski's graduation in 1930, George Halas offered him $5,000 to play for the Chicago Bears. Halas recalled that he had never seen a more remarkable physical specimen. "He was six feet two inches and he weighed two hundred thirty-four pounds, and it was all—literally all—muscle, skin, and bone. He didn't have an ounce of fat on him. A lot of men have passed in front of me but none with a build like that man."

Bronko was a symbol of power and irresistible force, who battered his opposition out of the way with a robust arm, calling into play fearsome knees and shoulders when necessary, dragging his tacklers over the goal line with him at last resort. Ernie Nevers, another of the all-time greats, who played with him at Minnesota, recalled, "Tackling Bronko was like trying to tackle a freight train going downhill." Red Grange, his teammate with the Bears, said, "When you hit Bronk, it was like getting an electric shock. If you hit him above the ankles, you were likely to get killed."

Bear quarterback Gene Ronzani, who played with Nagurski during most of his professional career, testified: "Not only was he as big and strong as advertised and not only was he a humble fellow and an all-around good guy, but he was the second fastest man on the Bears. And his toughness! He had a bad knee and sometimes he would come limping back to the huddle. I'd ask him if he wanted a time out and he'd say, 'Time out? Hell no, let's play football.' Then he would slap his knee on either side with that big hand of his—slapping the cartilage back in place."

Nagurski played seven years of the sixty-minute game for the Bears, but turned to professional wrestling when Halas refused to raise his salary to $6,000. In 1943, at the age of thirty-five, he was coaxed out of retirement to play tackle for Chicago. In the final game of the regular season, he took over as fullback, carrying the ball seventeen times for eighty-four yards, scoring one touchdown, and setting up two others. The Bears won over the Cardinals, 35–24, and Nagurski said, "That game gave me my greatest kick out of football."

Grantland Rice, who observed that many coaches considered Nagurski the greatest player of all time, wrote, "He was a star end, a star tackle and a crushing fullback who could pass. I believe 11 Nagurskis could beat 11 Granges or 11 Thorpes."

George Halas,
Vernon Biever,
Photograph, Collection
of the photographer

GEORGE HALAS (b. 1895)

George Halas—player, owner, coach, and promoter, and "Papa Bear" of the Chicago Bears—nursemaided professional football through its formative years, keeping the game alive, sometimes, it seemed, by the sheer force of his will. "People think I invented the game of football," he told a lecture audience. "And I did."

In 1920, Halas persuaded the A. E. Staley Manufacturing Company of Decatur, Illinois, to sponsor a semiprofessional football team. After a year, Mr. Staley found the undertaking too costly and suggested that Halas take the team to Chicago. This was the franchise that became the Chicago Bears in 1922. Halas rented Wrigley Field and himself acted as right end, captain, coach, press agent, ticket seller, training-grounds keeper, and all-around handyman. As a player, Halas held a long-standing record when he ran ninety-eight yards for a touchdown. He attributed his speed to the fact that he was being chased by Jim Thorpe.

Few people in the early 1920s paid any attention to professional football. Papa Bear set about changing that, first by paying a publicist ten dollars to write an account of the game which he then personally distributed to the local newspapers. But what he really needed, he soon decided, was a star—a Babe Ruth of football. Who else but Red Grange! Halas knew that he was right when he watched the lines form around the block, waiting to buy tickets to

Grange's professional debut at Wrigley Field on Thanksgiving Day, 1925. In the years ahead, Papa Bear would hire many other superstars. He first spotted Bronko Nagurski at Minnesota, playing both tackle and fullback. Halas turned Sid Luckman, the Columbia star, from a single wing tailback into a quarterback who became a brilliant executioner of Halas's newly devised T-formation. The T saw its most spectacular use in the 73–0 win over the Washington Redskins in 1940. Because of the attention the game brought to the new formation, Halas regarded it as one of the most important matches in the history of football. It was said that the Bears had played a perfect game—but Papa Bear, after studying the films, spotted one missed scoring opportunity.

Even in the 1950s and 1960s, after the Bears had ceased to dominate the game and Green Bay and Baltimore were in the ascendancy, Papa Bear continued to sign some of the greatest players in the league. In 1965 Halas drafted both Dick Butkus and Gale Sayers, even though he had to pay in the vicinity of $150,000 for each of them plus bonuses for signing. At sixty-eight, with the help of defensive coach George Allen, Halas knew his eighth championship season in 1963, his first National Football League title since 1946.

Papa Bear was noted, throughout his long career, for running along the sidelines gesticulating and shouting if he disagreed with the officials. In 1968, when an arthritic condition made it difficult for him to walk, he stepped down as head coach of the Bears. He would have liked to have stayed one more year to see the team through their Golden Jubilee but, as he explained to the press, "I have always followed the ball—and the officials—up and down the field. A coach has to stay on top of the action to make decisions. I cannot do that any longer."

At eighty-six, George Halas still goes to his office every day. He remains as chairman of the board of the Chicago Bears and president of the National Football League. "There is more to do now than ever, and if it wasn't for this gimpy leg of mine, I'd still be running up and down the sidelines."

Halas at the 1964 Pro Bowl Game, Pro Football Hall of Fame

SAMMY BAUGH (b. 1914)

"For calm poise, for nonchalance under fire, no college passer has equaled the fabulous Baugh," wrote Pudge Heffelfinger in 1954, remembering Sammy Baugh's spectacular career at Texas Christian University, where he threw 599 passes in three varsity seasons, 274 of them completed. At 6'2″ and weighing about 175 pounds, "Slingin' Sammy" (the appellation came from a brief stint as a shortstop with the St. Louis Cardinals) was seemingly too fragile for the grunt-and-groan game that was then pro football. But the skinny kid with immense and powerful hands, who had taught himself aerial precision by throwing a football through a spare tire swinging from a tree limb, used the ubiquitous, audacious forward pass of college play to revolutionize a rather slogging, often scoreless game.

George Preston Marshall, owner of the Boston Redskins, in search of a player who might add fast-moving excitement to a team that was attracting few fans, approached Baugh in the same year that he decided to move the team to Washington. The Texan, unsure, as were most people, as to what professional football was all about, arbitrarily asked for a salary of $8,000 a year, and Marshall agreed. Later, Baugh said that if he had known that veteran members of the Redskins were making only about half of that amount, he would never have ventured such a figure.

Marshall—"The Magnificent One," he was called—thought about football in show-business terms and cast Baugh, who had been born in the railroad switching stop of Sweetwater, Texas, and whose father worked for the Atchison, Topeka and Sante Fe Railroad, in the role of a colorful Texas cowboy. "People up here are expecting to see a

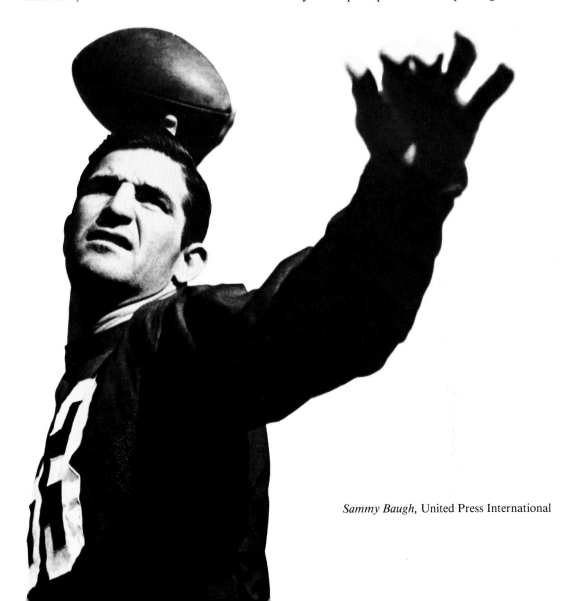

Sammy Baugh, United Press International

Baugh kicks the ball out of danger in a game against the Brooklyn Dodgers, November 1940, United Press International

Texan when you get off the plane, and I want them to see a Texan." Baugh arrived in Washington fitted out in a white ten-gallon hat and high-heeled cowboy boots.

In his rookie year with the Redskins, Baugh led them to a championship game, played against the Chicago Bears in snow and ice at Wrigley Field. In the next decade, the Redskins had a winning record each season, capturing five division titles and one more championship. For sixteen years as Redskins quarterback, Baugh not only maintained his reputation as the first of the great passers but also became known as a superlative place kicker and quick-kick specialist. Stepping back with his arm cocked, Slingin' Sammy would befuddle the opposition by suddenly booting the ball over their heads. "On punting ability alone he could turn a game topsy-turvy," wrote Arthur Daley of the New York *Times.*

Slingin' Sammy played with the Redskins until he was almost forty. And, if in the last years the team did not achieve championship status, it was not because of Baugh. By 1949 he was playing for his fifth pro coach and, what with the bickering between George Preston Marshall and the ever-changing Redskin coaches, the team fell apart around Baugh. "This is the most protection I've had all year," he jested at a gathering of FBI men.

When Baugh retired in December of 1952, *Times* sportswriter Daley noted that his "amazing career virtually spanned two gridiron generations, the era of the sixty-minute player and the era of free substitutions." Daley concluded: "The wiry Texan with the whiplash arm was the best passer of them all. This isn't merely an opinion. The record book proves it. Sammy has thrown more passes than anyone else, has completed more passes, has tossed more touchdown passes, has gained the most yardage (approximately thirteen miles), has the highest overall efficiency (56.6 per cent) and has the highest one season efficiency, an incredible 70.3 per cent."

Johnny Unitas,
Merv Corning,
Watercolor, 1975,
National Football
League Properties, Inc.

JOHNNY UNITAS (b. 1933)

At the time he retired in 1973, Johnny Unitas had attempted more passes (5,186), completed more of them (2,830), for more yardage gained (40,239), and more touchdowns by passing (290) than any other quarterback in the history of the National Football League. With Unitas calling the plays, the Baltimore Colts won forty-seven consecutive games, from December 9, 1956, through December 4, 1960—Johnny throwing at least one touchdown pass during each game. Twice the team had marched to the Super Bowl. Elected to the Pro Football Hall of Fame the first year of his eligibility, five years after his last game, the reticent Unitas said, "It is a great honor, but it is not the ultimate honor. It wouldn't have bothered me not to go in. Just being able to play the game for as long as I did was the ultimate." He played for eighteen seasons.

Eight hundred Colts fans—those loyalists whose enthusiasm Unitas once said made "going out in Memorial Stadium . . . like playing in an outdoor insane asylum"—were on hand at Canton, Ohio, to cheer the hero who had made Baltimore proud. Ever since a cool and confident Unitas, playing in the first sudden-death overtime game against the New York Giants in 1958, had brought the Colts eighty yards in twelve plays to the one-yard line, he had been the man with the golden arm; the greatest quarterback of them all, thought many.

Ironically, Unitas had risen to fame through a series of rejections. Notre Dame turned him down because, at 145 pounds, he seemed too slight for football. His hometown college at Pittsburgh refused him when he unaccountably flunked the entrance examination. After he had graduated from Louisville in 1955, he was drafted in the ninth round only to be cut before he even played in an exhibition game. But, although he went to work as a pile driver for a construction company, he was determined not to give up football. For six dollars a game, he played sandlot football with the semi-pro Bloomfield Rams in Pittsburgh. Picked up by the Baltimore Colts—mostly because he was a quarterback who did not cost anything—he soon got his chance when the starter, George Shaw, broke his leg in the fourth match of the season. An unprepared Johnny Unitas flubbed through his premiere game but, by the following week, he was ready to demonstrate his winning ways. "He is uncanny," Vince Lombardi said of Unitas, "in his abilities, under the most violent pressure, to pick out the soft spot in a defense." In the twilight of his career, his formidable image still hung on. Miami middle linebacker Nick Buoniconti observed, "With Unitas, it's scary. He seems to know what you're going to do before you do."

A new Colts management, who wanted to rebuild the team with younger players, traded the thirty-nine-year-old Johnny Unitas to the San Diego Chargers in 1973. As Johnny U. played his last game for Baltimore, a plane passed over the stadium pulling a banner which read "Unitas we stand."

Unitas, "The Man with the Golden Arm," Walter Iooss, Jr., Photograph, 1972, Sports Illustrated

VINCE LOMBARDI (1913–1970)

"I will demand a commitment to excellence and to victory, and that is what life is all about."
Thus spoke Vince Lombardi, who brought to football a religious fervor. More than any
other individual, Lombardi symbolized the 1960s' obsession with professional football.

Lombardi had been lucky, he once told a reporter, that he had found a singleness of
purpose early on. From the time he began to coach at St. Cecilia's High School in Engle-
wood, New Jersey, in 1939, he knew his life would be dedicated to football. He was forty-
six, however, before he had the chance to become a head coach beyond the high-school level.

When Lombardi's opportunity came, it was with the worst team in football at the
time—the Green Bay Packers, who had won but one game during the previous season.
Lombardi set about instilling professionalism. He made practice so difficult and demanding
that the games would often seem easy in comparison. "This is a violent sport. To play in this
league, you've got to be tough—physically tough and mentally tough." Defensive tackle
Henry Jordan explained, "He pushes you to the end of your endurance and then beyond it.
If you have a reserve he finds it." Said Lombardi: "You're going to have to live with pain.
If you play for me, you have to play with pain."

In their first game against the arch-rival Chicago Bears, the Green Bay Packers—already
taught by Lombardi that defeat was unthought of—won, 9–6. In a spontaneous gesture of
reverence, the players seized the coach who had screamed, bellowed, and damned them all
heartily, and carried him from the field on their shoulders. By the end of the second season,
Lombardi had propelled the Packers to a championship play-off game. In Lombardi's eight
years as Green Bay's coach, the team won five National League championships and the
first two Super Bowls.

Lombardi's brand of football was careful, not too different from the "grind-it-off-on-
the-ground way" he himself played when he was a guard on the Fordham line, dubbed "the
seven blocks of granite." The short pass, Lombardi conceded, was a part of the modern
game, but long passes he regarded as dangerous undertakings. Coach kept the offense as
simple as possible and concentrated on blocking and tackling. Lombardi's favorite maneuver
was to slip his running back through a hole in the defensive line—satisfied with a gain of five
yards on every try. A rival coach moaned, "You know what that damn team is going to do
on just about every play. But you can't stop them." A few snickered and called Lombardi
the William Gladstone of professional football, conservative to the point of boredom, but
most of America was spellbound. The Green Bay Packers sold out the stadium wherever
they played and attracted a following of millions through their frequent appearances on
national television on Sunday afternoon.

The announcement, in 1969, that Vince Lombardi had agreed to coach the Washington
Redskins was hailed as the "second coming." Washington hadn't had a winning team since
1955. Vince took command: "I want total dedication from every man in this room,
dedication to himself, to the team, and to winning. Winning is a habit, gentlemen. Winning
isn't everything, it's the only thing."

The first Lombardi season ended 7–5–2, and the team and the city were giddy with
anticipation that they were on the Green Bay trail. But Vince Lombardi, stricken with cancer,
died two weeks before the opening game of the new season. Redskin quarterback Sonny
Jurgenson, speaking to Packer guard Jerry Kramer, sighed, "I envy all you guys from Green
Bay. You had him for nine years. We only had him for one—just long enough for him to
educate us as to what it takes to win."

Jurgenson mused, "He used to tell us the world needs heroes, but I don't think he ever
realized what a big hero he was himself."

◄ *Vince Lombardi after the Green Bay Packers' victory over the Oakland Raiders in the Super Bowl,*
Neil Leifer, Photograph, 1968, Sports Illustrated

Jim Brown, Tony Tomsic, Photograph, 1957, Sports Illustrated

JIM BROWN (b. 1936)

Jim Brown may well be considered the most extraordinary of the running backs. He was "superhuman," remembered Chuck Bednarik, who, as middle linebacker for the Philadelphia Eagles, tried often to stop him. "He had finesse, ability, power—sheer power and desire; above all, he had desire." Six-foot-two and weighing 230 pounds, Brown was "physically gifted," combining size, strength, agility, and speed. Shaking off tacklers with his powerful thighs, he ran right through the linebackers and over the defensive backs. He had superlative balance, and his feet were never far off the ground—it was almost impossible to knock him down.

As a student at Long Island's Manhasset High School, Brown showed himself to be the consummate athlete—excelling in baseball, basketball, football, track, and lacrosse. The alumnus who steered him to Syracuse University was himself a lacrosse enthusiast. Brown's first two years of college football were rocky—he almost quit during his sophomore year when he was relegated to the second team—but before he graduated he had to his credit 2,091 yards gained and twenty-five touchdowns.

A first-round draft choice of the Cleveland Browns in 1957, Jimmy Brown was moved from halfback to fullback. He played for nine seasons, in seven of which he gained more than 1,000 yards. At the climax of his career, in 1963, he reached 1,863 yards. Used for carrying the ball more than most fullbacks—thirty-five times or so in a game—he was also

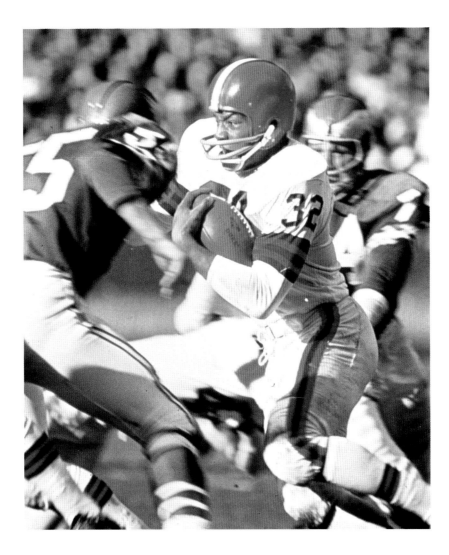

Brown—one of football's greatest running backs, Neil Leifer, Photograph, 1964, Sports Illustrated

said to be the highest-paid football player of his time, commanding a salary of $45,000. Coach Paul Brown explained, "When you have a thoroughbred you run him. That's what he gets paid for."

Brown was remarkable also for his durability. He survived 118 regular-season games, one divisional play-off, and three championship games with no injury of consequence. Brown explained: "By the time I was in pro ball, I figured that if I was going to make it against guys who outweighed me sixty or seventy pounds, I was going to have to develop something extra, something more than sheer muscle and flashy footwork. I was going to have to outthink the opposition. I would say that I credit eighty percent of the success I had to the fact that I played a mental game. . . . My game pivoted on having planned ahead of time every move I intended to make on the field."

Brown, at thirty, retired on top. Discussing his reasons for leaving football in favor of a movie career, he said, "Pride had a lot to do with it. I think a man ought to be remembered first of all as a great champion, à la Rocky Marciano, à la Otto Graham." Brown loved the game, and he acknowledged that it changed his life. "Otherwise I could have been some kind of gangster. I led a gang when I was a kid. . . . Football has done a lot for me, but if I hadn't had a talent it couldn't have done one thing. So Jim Brown and football have given to each other."

Gale Sayers on the verge of an explosive 1969 run, United Press International

GALE SAYERS (b. 1943)

Gale Sayers, said *Ebony* magazine, verbalizing the excitement of the running back's liquid style, "glides with the skill of a wave-riding surfer and accelerates faster than a souped-up Ferrari." Red Smith noted, "He wasn't a bruiser like Jimmy Brown, but he could slice through the middle like a warm knife through butter."

The Kansas-born Sayers first became a football star at Central High School in Omaha, Nebraska. Avidly recruited by nearly a hundred colleges, he elected to attend the University of Kansas. Twice the consensus choice for All-American, he was the coveted draft pick in 1965. Lamar Hunt of the American League's Kansas City Chiefs and George Halas of the National Football League's Chicago Bears both vied for his talents. Halas, notable for his thrift, was forced to offer, as he later remarked, more than he used to pay an entire team. He never regretted it. Before Sayers had completed his first professional season, Halas rated him among the Bear immortals—in the same class, he told the press, as Red Grange and George McAfee.

Sayers's rookie year was well-nigh incredible. In the December 12 game against the San Francisco 49ers, he ran eighty yards for a touchdown and then added five more, the last on an eighty-five-yard punt return. By the end of the year, he had scored twenty-two touchdowns, more than any other person in the history of the National Football League. "We knew he was good," said Sid Luckman, then an assistant coach with the Bears, "but this boy has turned out to be sensational." Telegraphed Ernie Nevers, who first set the six-touchdown game record in 1929, "Congratulations on the greatest one man performance I've ever witnessed on a football field. Your brilliance will long be remembered in this sport."

Sayers scored touchdowns in a surprising variety of ways, and seemed to do it effortlessly. Until he gathered the ball in his hands, he had a deceptively lethargic look. Vince Lombardi, chagrined after a Green Bay Packer loss to the Bears, 31–10, in 1965, acknowledged, "Sayers outran us! We misjudged him at least half the time. He's a great back. Better than we could have suspected." Exulted "Papa Bear" Halas, "He can lull you into thinking he is going at top speed, and then turn up another notch and be gone before you know it."

Sayers's prowess defied analysis. John David Crow, running back of the 49ers, could only say: "I wish I had the vocabulary to describe Sayers. He's a great, great football player, at a very young age. He's got quickness and speed, but he has something else that a great back must have. He has a sense of football, a feel for the game."

To Sayers it was just instinct. "I have no idea what I do. I hear people talk about dead leg, shake, change of pace and all that, but I do things without thinking about them."

In the middle of Sayers's fourth season with the Bears, the ligaments of his right knee were torn, and it was feared that his speed and agility might never be the same again. After surgery and an intense program of exercise, he rejoined the team in time for the 1969 season. He came back with assurance, leading the league in rushing with 1,032 yards and scoring eight touchdowns. His performance won him the Football Writers Association George S. Halas Award as the most courageous player in the sport. The next year, however, he injured his left knee. Before the beginning of the 1972 season, Sayers realized that he could not continue. At twenty-eight he retired. "His days at the top of his game were numbered," wrote Red Smith, "but there was a magic about him that still sets him apart from the other great running backs in pro football."

Sayers at Kansas University, 1963, United Press International

O. J. Simpson,
Andy Warhol, Acryl-
ic and silkscreen on
canvas, 1979,
Richard L. Weisman

O. J. SIMPSON (b. 1947)

In 1973, O. J. Simpson broke Jim Brown's ten-year record for the most yards gained by rushing in a single season when he passed the 1,863 mark and reached the incredible 2,003 statistic. When it was over, O.J. refused to meet the press without his teammates. "I want to introduce the cats who've done the job for me all year," Simpson said as he took the time to say a few words about each man in the offensive line. The gesture was typical of the grace and style which O.J. brought to the violent and competitive world of football.

Raised in San Francisco, Simpson graduated from high school with honors in football but a grade average too low for admission to a four-year college. After two years at junior college, he was accepted by the University of Southern California, where he led the Trojans to a Rose Bowl championship and set records for ball carrying and yards gained in a single season.

The will-o'-the-wisp runner was better even than Red Grange, thought pro-football scouts as they pronounced O.J. a combination of Jim Brown and Gale Sayers, the best running backs in the history of college football. When the data on the 1969 college stars for blocking, tackling, receiving, speed, quickness of reflexes, toughness, mental alertness, personal character, and judgment were fed into the computer, O.J. scored 0.5, the highest rating ever achieved.

The Buffalo Bills, as the lowest-ranking team in professional football, had the first draft choice, and they wanted O.J. badly enough to pay him a reported $100,000 a year. Although Simpson was never able to bring the impotent Bills any further than one National Football League play-off game, he proved to be a box-office attraction second to none save Joe Namath. Buffalo's dilapidated War Memorial Stadium held less than 46,000 spectators, but before the advent of O.J. it was rarely filled. Simpson's freewheeling broken field running guaranteed the thrills that brought the crowds that caused a new stadium to be built. "The House that O.J. Built," Rich Stadium, seated 80,000 and, with O.J. to watch, it was jammed to capacity.

The fans fell in love with O.J. as a running back, but soon they were also captivated by his great warmth and cheerfulness. Even those who never followed football came to recognize the articulate young man with the dazzling smile who jumped hurdles on his way to rent a car.

In 1978 Simpson, who wanted to return to his hometown of San Francisco, was traded, at his own request, to the San Francisco 49ers. "As a kid I always prayed and hoped to be a member of the 49ers." However, by the time O.J. got the opportunity, the team was touching the bottom of the league, and he himself, slowed down by three knee operations, was past his prime. Nonetheless, the 49ers felt that Simpson was well worth his more than $700,000 in yearly salary. Owner Edward DeBartolo, Jr., told the press, "I'd do it again in a minute. I have the utmost and highest respect for him, more than for anyone I've ever met. He's giving us everything he has, his guidance, his leadership."

O.J. retired in 1979 after eleven seasons, an exceptionally long career for a running back. In the last game before the home town, he displayed a final flash of his fabled brilliance, sprinting around the left end for a first down. "Juice! Juice! Juice!" roared the fans in appreciation. "For him to break back on the pursuit as he's done so many hundreds of times and then to be taken out of the game with the crowd receiving him like that," said 49er Coach Bill Walsh, "it's the ideal conclusion of his career here."

Simpson at the exact moment he broke the long-held NFL rushing record of Jim Brown, December 1973, Neil Leifer, Photograph, Sports Illustrated

283

JOE NAMATH (b. 1943)

Joe Namath was football's greatest newsmaker, sometimes on the field but more often off it. His perfect spiral passes, described as having "an elegance, a flair, an esthetic rightness about them," fascinated Americans. Even more fascinating was "Broadway Joe's" swinging lifestyle. "Boats. Planes. Cars. Clothes. Blondes. Brunettes. Redheads. All so pretty. I love them all." Few would dispute his reputation as "America's sexiest sports personality ever." As Namath said, in one of his most memorable television commercials, "If you've got it, flaunt it." And the more Joe flaunted it, the more America's attention was riveted on the upstart American Football League.

"I needed to build a franchise with somebody who could do more than just play," said Sonny Werblin, president of the New York Jets, explaining how it was that he had come to hire Joe Namath. Werblin watched him play for Alabama in the 1965 Orange Bowl game when, in pain from the first of his knee injuries, he threw a series of precision passes that almost defeated the favored Texas team. The former show-business talent agent said, "I don't know how to define a star, but I knew Joe had what it takes when he limped off the bench that night and seventy-two thousand people moved to the edge of their seats."

Namath was drafted on the first round by both the Jets and the National Football League's St. Louis Cardinals, and to get him Werblin had to offer a three-year package that included a salary of $387,000 and a Lincoln Continental convertible, making Namath the highest-paid rookie in the history of professional football. The week after the signing, the Jets sold two hundred thousand dollars' worth of tickets for the following season. Nonetheless, the Namath contract negotiation hastened the merger of the two leagues lest the recruiting wars bring bankruptcy to them both.

Joe Namath's football career was dominated by what became known as THE KNEES. Even before he played his inaugural professional game, *Time* magazine, on February 5, 1965, devoted its Medicine section to the first of his many operations. The weakness in his legs, and other injuries, which included a broken wrist and a shoulder separation, severely limited his career.

A Namath caricature, David Levine, Pen-and-ink drawing, Private collection

Before his knees gave out, Namath had one great season, which came to a climax at Super Bowl III, played in Miami on January 12, 1969. The Jets were 18-point underdogs against the Baltimore Colts. Joe played the most brilliant game of his career—twenty-eight passing attempts, seventeen completed—and carried the Jets to a 16–7 win, the first Super Bowl victory for the American Football League. Namath, it was written, had called "a near perfect game." New York gave him a hero's welcome and the key to the city.

Werblin had been right about Namath's star quality. Even after the Jets ceased to be a winning team (in 1970 they were 4–10; in 1973, 4–10; in 1974, they lost seven of the first eight games), Joe Namath continued to attract the fans. During his entire professional career, he played on only three winning teams. But, whether the season was win or lose, his commercial career flourished as had no other athlete's before or since. During the mid-1970s, he appeared constantly in TV endorsements. He made his first movie in 1970. It and two subsequent films were not well-received, but he continued to be fascinated by Hollywood and left the Jets in 1977 to play with the Los Angeles Rams. After four regular-season games, he was demoted from starting quarterback, and his one-year contract was not renewed. Henceforth he has determined to concentrate on his acting career. Asked to compare football with the entertainment business, Joe replied, "A lot of people don't realize that football is a sport that is choreographed, it's carried out by a group of people in front of a live audience; it's a live performance, and the other side isn't trying to help you one bit."

285

◄ *Joe Namath,* Neil Leifer for Sports Illustrated, Photograph, 1974, Collection of the photographer

LENDERS TO THE EXHIBITION

Albany Institute of History and Art
Malcolm Alexander
Athletic Association of the University of
    Illinois
Atlanta Athletic Club
The Atlanta Braves National League
    Baseball Club
Augusta National Golf Club, Georgia
Baseball Hall of Fame and Museum, Tokyo
Basketball Hall of Fame, Springfield,
    Massachusetts
Thomas Hart Benton and Rita P. Benton
    Testamentary Trusts
Vernon J. Biever
Bernice P. Bishop Museum, Honolulu
Borg-Warner Corporation
David A. Boss, National Football League
    Properties, Inc.
Boston Public Library
Brockton Historical Society, Massachusetts
Joe Brown
Don Budge
Dick Button
Calumet Farms, Lexington, Kentucky
Jim Campbell
Capricorn Galleries, Bethesda, Maryland
Mr. and Mrs. Robert J. Chambers
Dwight Chapin
Chicago Historical Society
Rich Clarkson
Robert Coleman
Mr. and Mrs. Burton Cooper
Elaine de Kooning
Detroit Historical Museum
Roy Gene Evans
Fair Grounds Race Track, New Orleans
Ralph Fasanella
Louis Felice
Nate Fine

John A. Fitzsimmons
John Philip Foster
Free Library of Philadelphia
Mrs. E. H. Gerry
Greentree Stables
John Groth
Hall of Fame of the Trotter, Goshen,
    New York
Robert T. Handville
Heritage Plantation of Sandwich,
    Massachusetts
Mrs. Thomas Hitchcock
Robert E. Hood
Gary Hoover
Humanities Research Center, University
    of Texas at Austin
Indiana Historical Society, Indianapolis
Indianapolis Motor Speedway
    Hall of Fame Museum
International Speedway Corporation,
    Daytona Beach, Florida
International Sports and Games Research
    Collection, University of
    Notre Dame Libraries
International Swimming Hall of Fame,
    Fort Lauderdale, Florida
Mr. and Mrs. Walter M. Jeffords
Fred Kaplan
Kean Archives, Philadelphia
Keystone Junior College, LaPlume,
    Pennsylvania
Mr. and Mrs. Barron U. Kidd
Jack Kramer
Stanley Kramer
Neil Leifer
Library of Congress
Manufacturers Hanover Trust, New York City
Lou Marciano
Peter Marciano

Mr. and Mrs. Robert Mathias
Willie Mays
Louis K. Meisel Gallery, New York City
Cornelius C. Mershon
Harry C. Meyerhoff
Minneapolis Institute of Arts
Tim and Karen Morse
Mr. and Mrs. Emil Mosbacher
Donald Moss
Musée du Sport, Paris
Museum of Cartoon Art, Port Chester,
    New York
Museum of Fine Arts, Springfield,
    Massachusetts
National Art Museum of Sport, New Haven,
    Connecticut
National Baseball Hall of Fame and Museum,
    Inc., Cooperstown, New York
National Football League
National Gallery of Art, Washington, D.C.
National Museum of American History,
    Smithsonian Institution
National Museum of Racing, Inc., Saratoga
    Springs, New York
New York Yacht Club, New York City
Patrick O'Brien
Ohio State University Libraries
Francis Ouimet Caddie Scholarship Fund, Inc.
Palm Beach Polo and Country Club, Florida
Peabody Museum of Salem, Massachusetts
Larry Pelliccioni
Richard Petty
Philadelphia Museum of Art
Walter Probst
Pro Football Hall of Fame,
    Canton, Ohio
Prorodeo Hall of Champions and Museum of the
    American Cowboy, Colorado Springs, Colorado
Racquet and Tennis Club, New York City

Ken Regan / Curt Gunther Camera 5
Robert Riger
Ring Boxing Hall of Fame, New York City
Mr. and Mrs. Albert Ritzenberg
The Jackie Robinson Foundation, Brooklyn,
    New York
Stanley Rosenfeld
Daniel Schwartz
The Science Museum, London
Lorne Shields Cycling Collection,
    Ontario, Canada
Spectrum Fine Art Gallery, New York City
The Sports Collectors' Store, Chicago
Sports Illustrated
The Sports Immortals Museum Collection,
    Joel Platt, Director
Springfield Art Museum, Missouri
William M. Stuart
Gail Thorpe
Grace Frances Thorpe
Jim Thorpe Home, Oklahoma Historical
    Society, Yale, Oklahoma
Janet Camp Troxell
Daniel S. Turner
United States Figure Skating Association,
    Colorado Springs
United States Golf Association, Far Hills,
    New Jersey
University of Chicago
University of Pennsylvania, Lloyd P.
    Jones Gallery
Richard L. Weisman
Whitney Museum of American Art, New York City
Dennie and Ina Williams
World Golf Hall of Fame, Pinehurst,
    North Carolina
Yale University Art Gallery
Yale University Library
. . . and various other private collections

PICTURE CREDITS AND PERMISSIONS

(by page number)